Count Tadasu Hayashi

From a photograph

The Secret Memoirs of
Count Tadasu Hayashi
G.C.V.O.

Edited by

A. M. Pooley

With Portraits and a Map

AMS PRESS
NEW YORK

Reprinted from the edition of 1915, London
First AMS EDITION published 1969
Manufactured in the United States of America

Library of Congress Catalogue Card Number: 72-93536

AMS PRESS, INC.
NEW YORK, N.Y. 10003

Contents

Contents

Illustrations

INTRODUCTION

I

The Career of Count Hayashi

HAYASHI TADASU was born in the second month of the third year of Kaei (1850), at Yedo. His father, Sato Taisen, was a native of the village of Kozu in the feudal fief of Sakura, where he had been adopted into the family of Hayashi Kaisha under the name of Hayashi Dokai. He followed his adoptive father's profession of physician, and became one of the best-known doctors of the pre-Restoration period, rising to the post of body-physician to the Shogun.

At an early age the young Hayashi, in company with Ito Masunosuke, was placed in the house of an American missionary at Yokohama, where he quickly learned to adapt himself to the ways of the "barbarians" and acquired a good grounding in the English language.

In 1866, on the recommendation of Sir Harry Parkes, the *bakufu* decided to make an

3

experiment by sending a number of students to England, instead of to Russia and the Netherlands which had hitherto been the foreign lands selected for Government students. Thanks to his father's influence at the Yedo Court young Hayashi was amongst the number chosen for this trial.

The party consisted of fourteen in all, and several of its members, as Hayashi himself, Toyama Shoichi, later Minister of Education, and Kikuchi Dairoku, now Baron Kikuchi, made names for themselves during the Meiji Era. Baron Kikuchi, who at that time was only twelve years old, is the only surviving member of the party.

Thanks to the arrangements made by Sir Harry Parkes, the party was enabled to travel to England on board an English warship returning from the Far East, the lads being placed under the charge of the chaplain, Mr. Lloyd. The voyage lasted from September, 1866, to January, 1867.

On arrival in London the British Foreign Office instructed Mr. Lloyd to take charge of the young men, and his first duty was to find accommodation for them. He made arrangements for them to lodge together in a house in Baker Street, but this did not suit Hayashi's views. He pointed out to their tutor that if they all lived together they would talk only Japanese and would live in Japanese style as much as possible, from force of habit. As a result they would neither acquire fluency in the English language nor acquaintance with English manners and customs, the two objects of their sojourn.

Mr. Lloyd, however, was unable to alter a situation which had the benediction of the authorities, but suggested that the boys should themselves draw up a petition to the Secretary of State. Hayashi took up this proposal with enthusiasm, and drafted his first diplomatic document, setting out his views, and requesting permission for the party to separate and to live in different private families. The petition was in due course acknowledged and granted.

The next move was to obtain some proper English education, and for this the students entered University College School in Gower Street, in the autumn of 1867.

Before they had been there many months, however, news arrived from Japan of the outbreak of the Restoration movement, and the Tokugawa officials summarily recalled the whole party.

When they arrived in Paris they found that the order for recall had been unaccompanied by funds to pay for their passages, with the consequence that the fourteen were stranded there with their clothes, and the revolvers and military equipment which they had bought in London.

Fortunately, a relative of the Shogun, Toku- gawa Minbunotayo, the Lord of Mito, was at that time in Paris, and in his suite was a gentleman who has since become famous as Japan's leading financier, Mr. (now Baron) Shibusawa. He arranged for the young men to return to Yokohama by the French mail- packet.

The party arrived in Japan just after the smashing defeat of the Tokugawa army at the battle of Uyeno. Hayashi at once pro- ceeded to Hakodate, where he joined the remnants of the Shogunate forces, which had gathered there round Admiral Enomoto, the staunchest of the Tokugawa retainers. He seems to have fought strenuously at both the battles of Hakodate and Masumae, but after the dispersal of the Shogunites he was taken prisoner and thrown into a dungeon to await execution, as he believed.

Although the real driving force behind the Restoration was the ambition of the great *daimyos*, especially those of Satsuma and Choshu, who had been kept in subjection by the Tokugawas, the Imperialist leaders were too far-sighted to imperil the future of the monarchy behind which they intended to establish their own oligarchy, by inhuman treatment of the enemy, although such would have been fully in accordance with the customs of the land. As soon, therefore, as the country had settled down under the new régime the imprisoned supporters of the Shogun were released, and Hayashi was not less fortunate than his fellows.

When the Emperor was safely on the throne a mission under Prince Iwakura was sent to the various Powers to announce the new order of things. Thanks to his knowledge of English, Hayashi was attached to this mission as interpreter, with the rank of a second secretary.

His connexion with it terminated rather suddenly whilst in London, owing to a piece of impertinence and disobedience on his part. Prince Iwakura being entertained by some personage expressed his delight at an apple, which he ate for lunch. His host on his departure presented him with a basket full of similar apples, which the Prince ordered Hayashi to dispatch to Japan. Realizing that the apples by the time of their arrival in the Far East would be unfit to eat or even to look at, Hayashi suggested to his fellow-secretaries to eat up the fruit and say nothing about it to the Prince. No sooner said than done! But, unfortunately, the Prince had either a longing for the apples or else a suspicion of Hayashi, for he asked on the following day if the fruit had been dispatched. The nervousness of the secretary whom he questioned aroused further suspicion, and eventually he learned the premature fate of the fruit. His rage was intense, and his first impulse was to send Hayashi back to Tokio in disgrace.

Fortunately, it happened that the Government in Japan hurriedly recalled Marquis Kido, the second envoy, and at his request Hayashi was transferred to his suite and returned to Japan, at least not out of favour.

About 1874, he was appointed interpreter to the Kanagawa Prefectural office. Mr. (later Count) Mutsu was then the Governor of Kanagawa-ken and was much struck by the tact displayed by his subordinate in handling the many difficult questions which arose between the foreign communities and the local authorities. Mutsu strongly recommended Hayashi to enter the diplomatic service and obtained for him an appointment in the Japanese Legation at London.

On his return to Japan he re-entered the service of the Kanagawa Prefecture, but was subsequently appointed Secretary of the Industrial Bureau, and in 1886 he became Secretary of the Imperial Household Bureau. Both these appointments he seems to have owed to the patronage of his former leader at Hakodate, Viscount Enomoto, who, like the great majority of the Shogun's followers, had entered the Imperial service.

In 1889, Hayashi was appointed Governor of Hyogo-ken, a post which he filled with considerable distinction.

With the grant of a constitution, the popular demand for the revision of the foreign treaties became insistent, and Mutsu, who had become Minister of Foreign Affairs, realized the advantage of having someone in the Gaimusho well acquainted, not only with the matters to be discussed, but with the foreign attitude regarding those matters. There was certainly nobody more suitable than his former assistant at Kanagawa, and, accordingly, in 1891, Hayashi left the Provincial Government to enter the Central Government as Vice-Minister of Foreign Affairs.

That he occupied this post with conspicuous success is a matter of history. Mutsu has left it on record that his achievement in obtaining the revision of all the most important of the foreign treaties was principally due to the indefatigable labours and the unfailing good sense and tact of his colleague.

It was at this time that the beginnings of the feud between Hayashi and Viscount Aoki occurred. Aoki, who was Japanese Minister at Berlin, was sent specially to London to conduct the negotiations with Lord Kimberley for the revision of the Anglo-Japanese Treaty, which terminated successfully in 1894. Hayashi had the opinion that in agreeing to the probationary clause Aoki rather let Japan down. However this may be, and it seems that Aoki really had no alternative but to accept the British terms, these two considerable statesmen were ever after on the coolest terms. The differences between them were very marked. Hayashi was, of course, very pro-British, Aoki by his marriage and long residence in Berlin was equally pro-German. Aoki was a Yamagata-Katsura man, Hayashi had no political or clan associations. The crisis in their relations came in 1907, when Hayashi summarily recalled Aoki in connexion with the American negotiations over the immigration question, a matter in which, as events proved, Aoki was right and Hayashi lamentably wrong.

Owing to Mutsu's failing health, Ito took charge of the negotiations at Shimonoseki, forcing from Li Hung-Chang the Liaotung clause, to which Mutsu was opposed. Hayashi remained in Tokio and was solely responsible for the negotiations for the Retrocession of Port Arthur. Mutsu, within a few days of the signature of the Shimonoseki Treaty, was stricken down by the painful disease which eventually terminated fatally, and had in fact left for America in search of a cure, before the Retrocession Edict was issued.

It was after the intervention of the three Powers that the remarkable programme printed as an Appendix to Chapter II was penned. In the light of subsequent events it must be acknowledged to be one of the most interesting documents of Far Eastern history.

No account of Hayashi's tenure of the Vice-Ministership should fail to notice his influence on the Japanese vernacular Press. His own connexion with Mr. Fukuzawa, the proprietor of the *Jiji Shimpo*, gave him a special interest in that paper, which became and remained until his death the organ of his views. Hayashi was the first Japanese statesman to realize and utilize the power of the *fudo* (pen-brush).

It was only during the Chino-Japanese War that the world at large began to take any serious notice of the Tokio papers. Previously they had been regarded as amusing broadsheets. By the intimate relations which he established with the leading journals, Hayashi laid the foundations of that extraordinary system of Press control which has since been one of the features of the Japanese bureaucracy.

It is a matter for regret that he did not confine his activities to the Press at home, and to such foreign papers in Japan as were willing to become the subsidized organs of the Government. But wherever he went he carried his Press Bureau with him. On his arrival at Pekin as Minister it was noted as a sign of his up-to-date methods that three accredited journalists were included in his official suite. The system which he initiated has since been carried to extremes, as was shown by the refusal a few years ago of the Minister of Finance to submit to the Diet the accounts of the I. J. Financial Commissioner in London, as the sums in question included various items for the entertainment of London journalists.

Hayashi was in May, 1895, appointed Japanese Minister at Pekin, and proceeded

to his post immediately in order to complete
the supplementary treaties and adjust matters preliminary to the evacuation of Manchuria. He arrived at Taku on June 11th,
being accorded a salute of fifteen guns and a
military parade. A warship had accompanied
his steamer as escort, and Li Hung-Chang
sent his yacht to convey him to land. He
arrived in Pekin on June 22d, and created from
the beginning a favourable impression, that
was enhanced by his English, which was
remarked as being without any accent.

Almost his first duty was to lodge a com-
plaint against high officials for gross disrespect.
In two official documents the Board of Censors
referred to the Japanese as "island barbarians," and Hayashi's remonstrance resulted
in an Edict of reprimand. The Japanese, of
course, now came under the most favoured
nation clause, and reaped the benefits of Sir
Thomas Wade's action, which made the use
of—I—(barbarians) by officials a breach of
treaty rights.

It cannot be said that Hayashi's tenure of
the Legation at Pekin was untroubled. The
Franco-Chinese Convention and the Chinese
Eastern Agreement provided opportunities
for his diplomatic talents, whilst the assassination of the Queen of Korea and the sub-

sequent intrigues of M. Waeber in that unhappy country undoubtedly caused him much anxiety.

It is interesting to remark that it is generally understood that Hayashi was ultimately responsible for the premature publication in 1896, by the *North China Daily News*, of the abortive Cassini Convention, although it should also be remembered that the Hong-kong correspondent of *The Times* had exposed the deal (but without a title) in October, 1895, when Reuter's semi-official denial from St. Petersburg was itself semi-officially contradicted by *Le Temps*.

In 1897, Hayashi, who had shortly after his arrival in Pekin been raised to the rank of Baron, was transferred to St. Petersburg, a post of which he has a good deal to say in the *Memoirs*. He was constantly occupied there in attempting to check the intrigues of Muravieff and Alexeieff to control Korea.

In 1899, Hayashi went to Tokio on leave, and whilst there was offered the post of Minister in London in succession to M. Kato. He had never laid aside his hopes of an alliance between England and Japan, and accepted the offer with alacrity, proceeding to his post in the following year.

He quickly established a reputation in

connexion with the Boxer rebellion, and it is
no secret that Japan's modest attitude in connexion with the settlement of that trouble
was largely inspired by her Minister in London, who saw in such a course a method of
soothing English susceptibilities and of laying
a foundation for future joint action in Far
Eastern affairs.

The crown of Hayashi's career was the
signature of the Anglo-Japanese Alliance in
1902, and its renewal on a broader basis in
1905. Not only did this bring him high
honours in his own country, but the promo-
tion of the Japanese mission in London from
a legation to an embassy. Hayashi was the
first Japanese Ambassador to the Court of
St. James, whilst Sir Claude MacDonald,
K.C.B., G.C.M.G., received reciprocal pro-
motion at Tokio.

In May, 1906, Hayashi was recalled to fill
the post of Minister of Foreign Affairs in the
first Saionji Cabinet, M. Kato having suddenly resigned office. To him fell the handling of the difficult *post bellum* situation in
Manchuria, the American Immigration question, and the general settlements of the Far
East after the upheaval of the war. He
negotiated agreements with France and Russia
for the maintenance of the *status quo*, and

concluded the Fishery and other conventions foreshadowed in the Treaty of Portsmouth.

It cannot be said that Hayashi's régime at the Gaimusho was very successful. How far this was due to himself and how far to circumstances it is difficult to say. Probably the blame must be divided. Hayashi came into office with strongly preconceived ideas, which appeared to run counter to the aims of the military part. Fully realizing the necessity of maintaining Japan's diplomatic credit, he insisted on the evacuation of Manchuria, which the soldiers strenuously opposed. In September, 1906, Hayashi retired, nominally on account of ill health, but really to avoid supporting a policy which he, like Kato, strongly disapproved. The Emperor ordered him back to office and he won the battle, but at the cost of the enmity of Prince Katsura and Prince Yamagata. That meant that he had against him Ito, Yamagata, and Katsura, the three most powerful figures in the Empire. Ito, who had always been pro-Russian and anti-British, had never forgiven Hayashi for his triumph in the matter of the alliance. Perhaps it was not for nothing that the Japanese used to say that Ito was more *zurai* (tricky) than *jozu* (clever).

But though Hayashi feared the impetuosity

and greed of the military party he was always willing to support it, even beyond the bounds of treaty rights or diplomatic honesty, when he saw the Japanese position in Manchuria menaced. The Fakumen Railway incident showed that he was ready to go to extreme lengths in support of the Manchurian plans of the militarists.

It was one of the ironies of fate that Hayashi, who made the alliance, should have been the Foreign Minister who had to demonstrate to the world how easily the pledges of maintaining the integrity and sovereignty of China could be evaded, and what a vacuous shibboleth the doctrine of the Open Door really was.

Nevertheless Hayashi's occupation of the Gaimusho was not without serious influence on Japan's future policy. Just as in 1895 he published a programme for the future conduct of the affairs of the country, so in 1907 he laid down the lines along which Japan must conduct her policy, to attain the object she has always held in view, the domination of the East.

The whole foundation of Japanese foreign policy as he enunciated it lay in simultaneous political and commercial penetration. The political ends were to be attained by the ever-

2

present threat of naval and military action, combined with a network of foreign agreements which, if they did not favour Japanese policy, certainly did not hinder it. The commercial ends were to be reached by the consistent pushing of Japanese subsidized financiers, shipping companies and traders for concessions. Commercial concessions were to lead to political control, just as political control was to include commercial concessions.

By a series of extraordinarily clever agreements Japan has been able to discount all Western obstacles which might arise in her path. The British, French, Russian, and American agreements with Japan have left that country practically a free hand in China, absolutely a free hand when their other engagements are considered. Germany did not count, for as far as Japan was concerned Germany was a negligible figure in Asia, until her position in Europe was finally assured. The Powers being therefore eliminated, Japan could proceed at leisure to nibble at China, either by conciliatory methods or by intrigue backed by force, as occasion might determine.

That was Hayashi's plan. That he made a mess of it in no way detracts from its merit.

It remains to-day the avowed policy of the Gaimusho.[1]

Where Hayashi made a mistake was in underestimating American interest in Korea and China. It is significant that the only serious error he made during his whole career was in connexion with the one country he had never visited, America. A Chinese proverb says: "A Hsuit'sai (B.A.) can manage the affairs of an Empire without leaving his room." A Japanese proverb says: "The cow thinks she can drink the river dry." Hayashi in dealing with the American questions was the cow of the Japanese proverb and the B.A. of the Chinese. He was too sure of himself and of his abilities. Both Aoki and Hayashi recognized that China was the crux of the difficulty between Japan and

---

[1] Hayashi would probably not have approved of the action of Japan in regard to China, reported at the time of going to press (April, 1915). He fully foresaw the dangers of unprovoked aggression, as is shown in his article on the Alliance in the Coronation number of *The Japan Times* (July 22, 1911). He wrote: "The value and importance of the Alliance will be unchanged, nor is there any doubt of its long continuance. The only point against which Japan must guard is a wantonly aggressive policy. On the contrary she must always adhere to a peaceful policy and endeavour to make the most of what she has gained so far and to promote her interests and development in a manner consistent with a pacific policy. If Japan should adopt a policy of wanton aggression the continuation of the Anglo-Japanese Alliance would be out of the question."

America. Aoki realized that if the problem of China were settled, Japan would be able to maintain her credit at Washington, for the school and immigration affairs were local difficulties on which it was uncertain even that Japan was in the right. Hayashi tried to shut out America from China by raising difficulties for her nearer home. He failed to realize that the Americans are a hard-headed business race, with a strong undercurrent of sentimentality. To their remonstrances with regard to Manchuria, he retorted by raising the school question. They came back with the immigration trouble, and Hayashi found that he had slung a boomerang, which returned in double quick time, bringing with it the whole of the credit which Japan had so carefully amassed in the States during fifty years past.

In a few months he killed the long-established friendship between America and Japan, and in place has been substituted on the one side an openly expressed dislike and suspicion and on the other a swelling hatred, which is only kept within manageable bounds by official repression.

After his recall Aoki intrigued with Katsura against Hayashi, and succeeded in excluding him from the Privy Council, a seat in which should have been the reward of his eminent services. The alleged cause of his exclusion, it will be recollected, was that he had become a Freemason, during his residence in London.

The Saionji Cabinet fell. It had never been intended to live. The ostensible causes of the fall were the finances, the real cause was the ambition of Katsura to return to power. But Hayashi left a legacy at the Gaimusho in a carefully considered policy of expansion, on the success of which the integrity or disintegration of China hangs, and the position of Japan amongst the Powers.

In the second Saionji Cabinet (1911–12) Hayashi held office *ad interim* as Foreign Minister, pending the return of Viscount Uchida from Washington, and permanently the portfolio of the Ministry of Communications.

During the military crisis in 1912, he steadfastly supported Marquis Saionji in his opposition to the Choshu demands. When the Cabinet resigned he was scathing in his denunciation of the Katsura clique. On his journey to Hayama he refused to occupy the special coach placed at his disposal by Baron Goto, his successor, travelling with his servants and family in an overcrowded second-class carriage.

He had for some time been suffering from acute diabetes, and from December, 1912, lived in strict retirement at his villa at Hayama. In June of the following year he was thrown out of a ricksha whilst returning from Kamakura, and fractured his thigh. He was removed to the Jutendo Hospital, where amputation was found to be necessary. He never properly rallied from the operation, and died in the hour of the Snake (10–11 A.M.) on July 10, 1913.

He was buried at the Aoyama Cemetery in the Foreign Office corner on July 13th.

It is pleasant to recall that his eminent services to Japan received a somewhat belated recognition from his sovereign, who donated Y.5000, a quite exceptional amount, to the cost of the funeral expenses.

Hayashi is said to have been rather soured towards the close of his career and is alleged to have complained because his services were not sufficiently requited. The claim seems to rest on but flimsy evidence. Hayashi was a man who was strictly honourable in all his dealings, and he scorned to use his official position for his private well-being. Like General Nogi he was deeply concerned at the course of events in Japan, and was much worried as to the future of internal politics.

He saw that the country was rapidly falling under the control of men whose only use for power was profit, their own not the nation's, and he was deeply grieved at the prospect. In a country where it has become the rule for statesmen to amass fortunes, he was a brilliant exception. He had no private means and never acquired any. When he retired he sold his house in Tokio and lived on his small pension in the country.

His death was a loss to Japan. He was one of the old school, one of the few statesmen remaining who had been trained in the atmosphere of the Restoration. He has been described as an *Edokko*[1] to the backbone; quiet and unpretentious, a scholar and a gentleman, he was a man of strong opinions, and a good fighter. An excellent host, a good conversationalist, he was an authority on art and music and an expert at *go*.

His favourite recreations were singing and dancing, and he was a patron of many of the leading *geisha*, whilst as a calligraphist his manuscripts and writings were highly prized.

---

[1] *Edokko*—a term used frequently by novelists to denote a special type of character, of which boldness, fortitude, chivalry, hospitality, high culture, and lavish prodigality were the principal traits.

II

Count Hayashi's Literary Work

THE late Count Hayashi published a novel in English (*For His People*, Harper, 1903), and also contributed the introductions to Mr. Alfred Stead's *Mysteries of China*, and to Mr. Arthur Lloyd's *Everyday Japan*.

The first of these was a romance dealing with a local episode in the feudal history of Sakura, the author's legal birthplace. Kinchi Sogoro, headman of Kozu, one of the villages on Lake Inoa, in the fief of the Lord Hotta, rouses his fellows against the tyranny of their feudal chief. Failing to obtain redress for their wrongs, Sogoro determined on the extreme and unforgivable step of appealing directly to the Shogun, counting the intervention of the *bakufu* on behalf of the peasants as worth more than the death which Hotta would mete out to him according to law for addressing the Shogun. Sogoro carried out his plan and actually succeeded in handing his petition to Tokugawa. He, his wife, and children were condemned to death, crucified and beheaded. In his last moments Sogoro vowed revenge and ordered his spirit to haunt Hotta till his family should be wiped out, a curse which was duly fulfilled.

Count Hayashi's object in publishing the story was to teach the West the spirit that animated his countrymen: presumably their persistence in a course once determined on, their revenge for slights and wrongs.

The novel is noteworthy for the excellent English in which it is written, which contrasts most favourably with the so-called "quaint" English with which Anglicized Japanese authors of to-day harass their readers. As a picture of pre-Restoration times *For His People* is without doubt a faithful likeness. The close connexion of the Hayashi family to Sakura and the Shogunate ensures that the descriptions of Yedo and the customs of the court and people are faithfully reproduced.

The introductions to Mr. Stead's and Mr. Lloyd's volumes are brief and to the point. In the former the reader is able to surmise the writer's profound knowledge of Chinese character. He practically summarizes the Chinese as necrologists, blind worshippers of a dead past, but he frankly admits the brilliance of that past, even though it is a hindrance to a decent present or future.

He says: "The essential feature of the political teaching of the great sages is the supreme importance attached to the individual morality of the ruler, and its prevailing spirit is that intense reverence for antiquity which constitutes the extreme form of conservatism."

"The Chinese mind was utterly enslaved by the influence of these doctrines, so that the idea of instituting a comparative study of political or ethical questions was banished therefrom."

"The inevitable result was careful preservation of a civilization acquired during a period of greater receptivity but a complete cessation of all further progress."

In introducing Mr. Lloyd's book, Count Hayashi emphasizes the important part Japan must play in Far Eastern affairs and the necessity of the world at large knowing everything possible about her. As is evident from parts of the *Memoirs* he fully realized the power of the pen, but he did not sympathize with the views of most of his colleagues, that books on Japan should reveal only the bright side of life in that country. He had mixed too much with foreigners, both in Japan and abroad, not to know that in every country there must be dark spots, and in every government some abuses requiring correction. As he says, "Fish do not see water," and the ability to "see ourselves as others see us" is as valuable a one in a nation as in individuals.

It has been asserted that if he had lived Count Hayashi would not have published his *Memoirs*. There is no evidence whatsoever for such a statement. He left explicit instructions that they were to be published. His whole course of life was a proof that he was not ashamed to criticize his nation. In a conversation I had with him in January, 1912, soon after I arrived in Tokio, he said: "Don't be afraid to handle thorns. It will be good for you and us!" He himself was not afraid, as his articles in the *Jiji Shimpo* on the Korean Conspiracy Trial and the prevalence of torture in prisons in Japan and Korea and on the fall of the Saionji Cabinet in 1912, fully show.

In Japanese, Hayashi published *Itarii Shi* (*History of Italy*), and a translation of Mill's *Political Economy*.

So far as I have been able to learn, Hayashi, on account of his official rank, rarely contributed signed articles to the Japanese Press, but he was practically responsible during many years for the attitude of the *Jiji Shimpo* on foreign questions, and wrote a great number of anonymous articles in that paper and in the *Chuo Koron*. The consistently high standard which the *Jiji Shimpo* has maintained on all matters of foreign policy and its out-and-out pro-British stand was in no small degree due to the relationship between its proprietor, M. Fukuzawa, and the diplomat.

I have referred on an earlier page to the connexion which Hayashi practically initiated between officialdom and the Press. It is a matter of the utmost importance. For many years the British and American Press have been so slovenly represented in Tokio, and indeed is so to-day, that the close connexion between the Government and the vernacular Press has been sadly overlooked. If it were realized that such institutions as the Bank of Japan, the Finance Department, and the Foreign Office have each their own organ of publicity, whilst every leading statesman has some paper wedded to his views, the naïve *démentis* of vernacular statements issued in London would not receive so much credence as they do.

After the fall of the second Saionji Cabinet, I travelled in the same carriage with the late

Count from Tokio to Yokohama. He was then on his way to his villa at Hayama. In the course of conversation he said that he would like to be younger, when he would adopt a journalistic career.

About a year later I was travelling from Oiso to Tokio in company with Baron Kato, the present Foreign Minister. Discussing the late Count, Baron Kato said that Hayashi had actually intended to enter journalism and had hoped to become a regular contributor on Japanese affairs to *The Times*, which paper had a year before lost the services, through death, of its veteran correspondent, Captain Brinkley.

The *Memoirs* which are published hereafter were written during 1902, 1903, 1906, 1907, and 1908. The intention of the late Count had been to write a history of Japanese diplomacy from the time when he began in 1871, "as a small potato of the diplomatic world," down to his retirement from office at the fall of the first Saionji Cabinet in 1908.

Such a work would have been, in fact, a complete history of the whole of that remarkable period of the Meiji Era, during which the enormous changes in Japan itself and in Japan's foreign relations occurred, which raised that country from being an unknown and rather discredited island to one of the Powers of the world.

Unfortunately, methodical as he was in his diplomatic work the Count was most unmethodical in his literary work. He obviously intended to base his history on his own diary and on the numerous articles which he contributed to the Press. He planned out the whole of the proposed volume but never actually wrote more than the chapters dealing with the Anglo-Japanese Alliance and the chapters dealing with his own tenure of the Foreign Office. Even these latter were not complete, for the portions dealing with the American Immigration question and with the Fakumen Railway are not available. This is a matter of considerable regret, as on both of these some pleasing indiscretions might from the circumstances of the case have been reasonably looked for.

In the *Memoirs* as they are published here certain material has been included which was not in the completed manuscript, but was contained in unfinished chapters or in articles contributed to the vernacular Press. It has been considered advisable to insert this material for the purpose of rounding off the Count's story.

From May, 1913, the *Chuo Koron*, a reput-

able but little known monthly review in
Tokio, began the publication of a series of
disjointed paragraphs which were described
as the reminiscences of a retired diplomat.

On July 29, 1913, the *Jiji Shimpo* began
to publish a series of articles embodying the
paragraphs from the *Chuo Koron* and entitled "History of the Anglo-Japanese Alliance." The paper announced that these
articles were narrative stories dictated by
Count Hayashi. The following day a second
article appeared which was much more de-
tailed in the information which it conveyed
and was obviously the diary of the late statesman. A footnote added by the editor stated
that the article was, in fact, a reproduction
from the diary of the late Count Hayashi
which had been placed at the disposal of the
newspaper by the executors, and that it was
proposed to continue its publication. On
the following day, July 31st, the *Jiji
Shimpo* announced that it had received the
following letter from the Japanese Foreign
Office:

"The matter under the heading of the 'History of the Anglo-Japanese Alliance' is considered objectionable, and you are requested
not to publish any more articles of the series.

I write this at the instruction of the Minister of Foreign Affairs.

(Signed) "YOSHIDA YOSAKU,
"*Confidential Secretary to the Minister of Foreign Affairs.*"

On August 21st, the *Jiji Shimpo* rushed out a supplement containing a summary of the continuation of the articles. It was immediately seized by the police and suppressed, and every effort made to prevent any translation of the same going abroad, both telegrams and letters being stopped. I was fortunate enough to smuggle a translation to London, where it was published and created no small surprise.

At that time it was not to be expected that any further parts of the *Memoirs* would be available, as the Foreign Office seized all the material which the Hayashi family or the *Jiji Shimpo* held, and extracted an undertaking that they would not countenance or encourage any further publication.

In October, 1913, I was approached by a certain Japanese, who held a manuscript written by Count Hayashi and specifically given by him to the owner with instructions for it to be published. The owner had obtained a loan on the manuscript, which was a wonderful example of calligraphy, and if I paid off the loan I could have the use of the manuscript. An undertaking was given me at the same time that the manuscript was the legal property of the gentleman in question. On receiving the manuscript I found a letter from Count Hayashi to the owner as follows:

"I give you this manuscript with the intention that you shall publish the same after my retirement from office or at some proper occasion.

(Signed) "HAYASHI."

I had the most important parts of the manuscript translated and my translations were on their way to London and Shanghai within forty-eight hours. A few days later I was able to borrow this manuscript again to complete and check my translation.

The day before the publication of the selected extracts, I was approached by a representative of the Hayashi family, who desired to suppress the publication. How they learned about it I never knew, but I suppose somebody talked. This gentleman informed me that they believed that the manuscript I had used was a copy made by

3

an employé of the *Jiji Shimpo*, and was very much surprised to find it contained material of which he had never heard, and was one of which the Hayashi family had no knowledge whatever.

To prevent any charge of breach of faith being made against any members of the Hayashi family or any members of the staff of the *Jiji Shimpo*, I addressed the letter given below to the Minister of Foreign Affairs. It is perhaps not a matter for surprise that I received no acknowledgment of it.

"H. E. BARON MAKINO,
    "H.I.J.M.'s Minister for Foreign Affairs,
    "Tokio.
"YOUR EXCELLENCY,
    "With reference to the continuation of the late Count Hayashi's *Memoirs*, which my company (Reuter's) are now publishing in London and Shanghai, I take the liberty of informing Your Excellency that no member of the Hayashi family nor any member of the staff of the *Jiji Shimpo* has had any connexion whatsoever with the same.

    "The manuscript from which I have had the advantage of working is one of which they knew nothing, and of the existence of which they were totally unaware.

"I write this letter in order that no charge of breach of faith may be brought against them.   In fact, they have done everything possible to prevent publication of the same.

"I am,
"Your Excellency's obedient servant,
(Signed) "ANDREW M. POOLEY."

To protect the reputation of the Hayashis and their friends I had a copy of this letter sent out to every newspaper in Tokio.

In April, 1914, I learned through Japanese friends that there was yet another manuscript in existence, actually in the possession of a pawnbroker.   I obtained access to this, and was enabled to compare it with the other material in my possession.   It was a very incomplete affair of some forty sheets, and but comparatively little of it was in a sufficiently finished state to be of value.   It consisted mostly of articles contributed to the Press.

The most interesting point in connexion with the suppression of the *Memoirs* is that on the day of King George's Coronation, Hayashi published a summarized and innocuous account of the negotiations for the Alliance in *The Japan Times*.   Three days later he published a more extensive and distinctly non-official version in the *Asahi Shimbun*, but did not sign it. This latter version created some interest, but was pooh-poohed by everybody as being a fiction of journalistic imagination. Even so shrewd a critic as *The Japan Chronicle* headed its translation: "What passes for history!"

III

The Chino-Japanese War

By the Treaty of 1885, known as the Tientsin Convention, signed by Li Hung-Chang and Count Ito, the relative positions of China and Japan towards China's vassal State, Korea, were defined. The final clause of the treaty stipulated that neither Power should send troops into Korea without notifying the other signatory. Each Power should have the right to send an equivalent number of troops to that sent by the other, in case either side should consider such a measure necessary.

The Tientsin Convention was regarded by Japan as a diplomatic triumph, annulling China's suzerainty over Korea, and giving Japan equal rights in that country. Nevertheless it did nothing to modify the strong dislike of the Korean Court and people for the Japanese, a dislike which was steadily fostered by the Chinese Resident, Yuan-Shi-Kai, and by the Russian Minister at Seoul, M. Pavloff, who in 1888 concluded the "Overland Commercial Treaty" with Korea.

37

The Japanese authorities had ever since that year been preparing to settle the Korean question by force of arms, in the event of a peaceable settlement proving impossible. The army and navy had been steadily improved both in material and personnel, and, as events were soon to show, had reached a remarkably high state of efficiency.

Nevertheless it is improbable that the Japanese statesmen would have pushed matters to a crisis in 1894, but for a fortunate concatenation of circumstances.

In February, 1894, a certain Kim-ok-In, a Korean political refugee, who had for some years been living in Japan, was enticed to Shanghai on the pretence of negotiating with representatives of the Korean Court, and was there murdered. Rumour was strong that the murder of Kim originated in the brain of Yuan-Shi-Kai. Whether this was so or not, his death removed from the scene a very useful pawn, on whom the Japanese Foreign Office had been able to rely as a go-between between itself and the Korean reformers. His murder was made the opportunity for the formation of a political association called the "Anti-Korean Association," which had for its avowed object the forcing of an active Korean policy on the Imperial Government. It was largely financed by semi-official institutions, and was kept in touch with the authorities by a certain Ryonosuke Okamoto, who has been well described as the stormy petrel of Korean politics.[1]

Owing to the intrigues of the "Anti-Korean Association" and the financial support accorded from Japan, the Tong-haks started an insurrectionary movement in Southern Korea towards the end of May, 1894. The insurrection in itself was of little importance, and there does not ever appear to have been any real danger to either the Korean dynasty or to the foreign residents of the country. Both China and Japan availed themselves of the terms of the Tientsin Convention to send troops into Korea, each country formally notifying the other of its intention. China took this step first. Li Hung-Chang undoubtedly was anxious not to send troops into Korea, and it was only after considerable delay that he deferred to the opinion of Yuan-Shi-Kai, who was naturally afraid that the Japanese forces would arrive first on the scene. There is little doubt but that both Li and Yuan were worked on by Russian influence, the former by Count Cassini and the latter by M. Pavloff, for neither of these extremely astute diplomats had any desire to see Chinese influence at Seoul replaced by Japanese domination. Li accordingly dispatched 3000 men to Asan. On

[1] Ryonosuke Okamoto was subsequently forced on the Korean Court as Military Adviser; he led the band of assassins who murdered the Queen of Korea in 1896. Later he was one of the leaders of the Japanese participating in the Chinese Revolution of 1911, and died at Shanghai in 1912.

June 9th a mixed division of 8000 Japanese troops landed in Korea, although, as *The Eastern World* of Yokohama pointed out, nothing had as yet happened in Korea to necessitate the dispatch of such a large force.

On June 16th the insurrection was declared to have been suppressed, and China notified Japan that she was about to withdraw her forces, and requested Japan to do the same.

A week later it became known that Japan had refused to comply with this proposal, and the situation between the two countries was declared by the Tientsin correspondent of *The Times* to be critical. On June 24th a Chinese squadron was ordered to Chemulpo. On the 25th a Japanese official statement claimed that the Tong-hak rebellion had not been suppressed, and alternatively that even if it had been steps must be taken to prevent a recurrence of the trouble and that such steps were of vital importance to Japan, as her economic interests in Korea were greater than those of China. A joint intervention and the establishment of a scheme of fiscal reform were proposed by Japan. China replied that it was contrary to traditional policy to interfere with the internal affairs of a vassal State, a reply that elicited the retort that unless China agreed to intervene, Japan would have to do so alone.

The Korean situation was, as a result of the Tong-hak trouble, favourable to Japanese policy. Conditions in that country, especially in the parts proximate to Japan, gave a nominal justification for intervention, even though the rebellion itself was but a poor thing as rebellions go, and without doubt fostered by Japanese. The internal situation in Japan was also not without its arguments in favour of drastic action. For many years the strongest movement in the political world had been that which demanded the revision of the Japanese treaties with foreign Powers, and the retrocession of the treaty ports. Cabinet after Cabinet had fallen on account of failure to accomplish this. It was perhaps unfortunate that coincident with the rise of the revision movement came the efforts of Count Itagaki to establish government by political parties. This at once made the question one of internal politics. The Diet, composed as to a large majority of men who had no knowledge of foreign affairs, and ignorant of the very A B C of politics, was unable to co-ordinate the expenditure of large sums of money on armaments with the continuation of extra-territoriality. This resulted in bitter fights between the Cabinet and the Parliament, and the period from December, 1893 to June, 1894, saw the dissolution of two Diets, the first of which only sat for a month, and the second for only eighteen days. The dissolution of both was due to the insistence by an Opposition more powerful than the Ministry on the pursuit by the latter of a strong foreign policy.

The large force thrown into Korea was primarily

a sop to popular feeling. The withdrawal of the expedition at the request of China would have had most serious results in Japan, for the situation would have resolved itself diplomatically into a *status quo ante*, whilst politically it would have meant ruin for Ito and Mutsu.

Besides the Korean situation and the condition of internal politics there was another impulse of which notice must be taken. Since 1893 Mutsu had been negotiating with the British Government for a revision of the Anglo-Japanese Treaty. The conduct of the negotiations had been entrusted to Viscount Aoki, Japanese Minister at Berlin. When the Korean crisis arose, the draft of the new treaty had been agreed upon by both sides, but Lord Kimberley refused to allow the new treaty to come into force until the codes had been revised and were operating satisfactorily. A revision of the treaty with Britain was a diplomatic success on which Ito could have justifiably demanded praise from the Diet. A revision, the action of which could be indefinitely postponed, would be worse than useless. On the other hand, a successful Korean campaign would not only unite all parties, but would distract public attention from the question of the treaty revision, and probably help forward the revision of the other treaties.

The above were the immediate reasons for Japanese action. There were, however, greater issues at stake than the future of Parliamentary

government in Japan or the Parliamentary future
of Ito or Mutsu. For years Japan had had the
run of every secret document in China. In 1882
the Board of Censors had raised in a memorial
to the Throne the problem of Korea. Chang-
Pei-Lun, afterwards the son-in-law of Li Hung-
Chang, in a very cleverly argued report, urged on
the Throne the necessity of China thoroughly
reforming her army and navy, finding a satisfactory
excuse for war with Japan, and then thoroughly
crushing the *wojen*, a contemptuous term for the
Japanese. He advanced reasons for the belief
that Great Britain and the Powers would support
China. This memorial was sent by the Throne
to Li Hung-Chang for his opinion. The Viceroy
approved in the main the argument for reforming
the army and the navy, but was more inclined to
believe that the Loochoo Islands would form a
better excuse for a war with Japan than the question of Korea. He thought, contrary to Chang-
Pei-Lun, that the European Powers would support
Japan against China.[1] The Japanese Foreign
Office had a copy of this memorial, and was consequently fully aware of the intention of China to
pick a quarrel one day with Japan and fight.
The Japanese Government had therefore for years
been preparing for the day, and was determined
itself to decide the time of the conflict. The late
Captain Brinkley, *The Times* correspondent in

[1] Appendix A.

Tokio, and a close friend of Count Ito, entirely endorses this view, both in the columns of his own paper, *The Japan Mail*, and also in the correspondence which he contributed to *The Times*. He says that Japan was prepared to the last button, and "as for cartridges, she has stacks more than she could possibly use in a war against China." He admits that Japan's actions were not dictated by philanthropy but were intended to transmogrify Korea into a profitable neighbour for Japan. "Japan," he writes, "was ambitious to annex Korea, but knew that her ambitions would be restrained by the Powers, and Japan fears nothing so much as European complications."

The manner in which Japan fomented trouble in Korea and fixed a quarrel on China was ugly, but at the worst she was only forestalling a similar course of action by China. Her policy was opportune in view of the situation at home and abroad, especially in China, where a closer *rapprochement* with Russia was being effected. After all, the Korean question as between China and Japan was *eine Machtfrage*. Japan forced the issue, and because she was prepared, whilst China had only talked preparation, she won.

From June 25th, when Japan declared her intention of continuing her intervention in Korea, matters became critical. Some doubt existed in Japan as to the attitude of the European Powers in the event of war breaking out. The Memoirs left behind by the late Count Mutsu give an account of the diplomatic conversations which took place in order to clear up this doubt. It is a matter for regret that the Japanese Foreign Office seized and destroyed as many copies of this work as it was able to, and forbade further publication of the same. It is from one of the few remaining copies that I obtained the following summary of these conversations.

There were only two Powers from whom Japan had to fear hostile action. They were Great Britain and Russia. Of these two the former was by far the more important, If Great Britain could be persuaded to maintain a neutral position it was highly improbable that Russia would take any steps beyond diplomatic representations. The first point to be elucidated was as to whether Great Britain had any secret agreement with China, which would necessitate her taking naval or military action on China's behalf.

The Japanese Minister in London was instructed to ascertain the views of Downing Street. The result of the interview was a warning to Japan that Great Britain would deprecate any outbreak of hostilities, and would most certainly refuse to tolerate any actions which infringed her own interests in China or the integrity or independence of Korea. The Japanese representative was instructed that this information was insufficient, and was ordered to try and obtain a further statement as to how far Japan could go without trespassing on the limits prescribed by Great Britain, limits which Mutsu described as being "very ambiguous." He was instructed to point out that Japan's only object was to obtain a settlement of the Korean question by reforming her internal administration. The reply to this was that Great Britain would weclome any amelioration of the internal conditions of Korea, but she would not be able to regard with indifference any material change in the foreign regulations of Korea, nor would she acquiesce in the transfer to Japan of any of the territorial possessions of the King of Korea. This very definite exposition of the British point of view was accompanied by the warning that any attempt of the Japanese to control the peninsula would certainly lead to Russian intervention, and possibly the seizure of a Korean harbour by Russia. On the receipt of the above statement Mutsu instructed the Japanese Minister at London to give a formal assurance to the British authorities that whatever the outcome of the existing situation, Japan had no intention whatsoever of seizing any Korean territory.

This assurance was very timely, as the general impression in foreign circles in the Far East was that Japan really wanted to grab Korea, or as Bishop Corfe more politely expressed it, "Japan only wants to annex Korea."

There was good reason for Japanese fear of opposition from Russia. Li Hung-Chang practically disclosed in his farewell speech to Count

Cassini that the dispatch of Chinese troops to Korea had been the result of the latter's advice, whilst the identical note presented on June 25th by the *corps diplomatique* at Seoul to Yuan-Shi-Kai, and M. Otori, the Japanese Minister, calling on both parties to withdraw their forces, was drafted by M. Pavloff, though it was nominally presented at the request of the King. China agreed immediately to the request, but Japan never answered the note.

On June 28th Li Hung-Chang issued the following manifesto:

"China is Korea's suzerain; she receives tribute and confers investiture, and therefore she owes protection to the vassal State. Accordingly at the King's request she dispatched troops to quell the Tong-hak rebellion, informing Japan thereof in accordance with the Convention of 1885, and engaging to withdraw her troops on the suppression of the rebellion. There was no need for the interference of Japan, though Japan, too, has the right to send troops to Korea.

"On the appearance of the Chinese forces the rebels dispersed. China now desires to withdraw from Korea, but Japan refuses to evacuate Korea simultaneously with China, and proposes joint occupation, administration of the finances, and the introduction of reforms. These are tasks which China cannot accept, though she is willing to join Japan and other nations interested in recommending the reforms necessary to the King of Korea.

"Japan's attitude threatens to cause a crisis in Eastern Asia and may prove dangerous to both countries, as well as deplorable to general commerce.

"The Viceroy, Li Hung-Chang, considers the action of Japan to be inconsistent with the law of nations, and with existing treaties. He will nevertheless endeavour to preserve peace without dishonour to China."

The reply of Ito and Mutsu to this protest was to present to the King of Korea a series of further demands, including the abandonment of Chinese suzerainty, the dismissal of the Chinese Resident, the reform of the civil, military, and legal systems, and the grant to Japan of certain railway, mining, and loan concessions.

Li Hung-Chang turned to Russia for advice. Russia was in no mind and in no condition to draw the sword to assist China, but she was willing to go as far as possible in moral support, in order to maintain the *status quo* in Korea. M. Hitrovo, the Russian Minister at Tokio, called on Count Mutsu and handed him a note in which the Russian Government expressed the point of view that China had explicitly fulfilled all the conditions of the Tientsin Convention; further, that she was prepared to evacuate Korea, and that Japan should do the same; further, that if Japan declined to follow this advice and a breach of the peace should be caused thereby, Japan alone could be held responsible. The Japanese Minister tried to draw M. Hitrovo, by asking him whether he was to understand by the last clause of the note that Russia was prepared to support China otherwise than diplomatically, but the Envoy only answered that he had no instructions beyond those contained in the note.

Mutsu was still in doubt as to how far Russia would go, when a quite unforeseen turn was given to events by a bellicose statement in the *Novoye Vremya*, that if Japan went too far, Russia would declare a joint protectorate over Korea with China. This brought Germany into the field, with a declaration that any attempt to introduce Russia into the settlement of the Korean question would result only in the creation of a Far Eastern Egypt, a threat which was followed by the dispatch of warships to the North Pacific.

On July 16th, the Anglo-Japanese Treaty was signed, and on the 19th the Japanese Minister in London informed Lord Kimberley that Japan would insist even by force on a satisfactory solution of the situation. As a result Lord Kimberley telegraphed to Rome, Berlin, Paris, and St. Petersburg, asking the Governments of the Powers to instruct their representatives at Pekin and Tokio to use all their efforts for the maintenance of peace. At the same time Mr. Gresham, the American Secretary of State, telegraphed to Mr. Dunn and Mr. Foster, the United States representatives at Tokio and Pekin, offering the services of the United States as mediator. These dispatches were held up by the Japanese authorities.

4

On July 22d, the King of Korea accepted the Japanese demands, contingent on the immediate evacuation of the country by Japan, a condition which was promptly refused. On July 23d, the Japanese troops in Seoul seized the person of the King, and in a riot which ensued killed a number of Koreans.

War was thereafter inevitable. Great Britain, with the view of limiting the area of hostilities, demanded, and Japan agreed, to the neutralization of Shanghai. The Kowshing incident immediately followed, and war was formally declared on August 1st.

The Retrocession of Port Arthur.

As Count Hayashi remarks, the action of Russia was by no means unexpected. The note of M. Hitrovo, before the outbreak of war, had clearly shown that Russia would side with China, and it is possible that only the death of Alexander III. and the assassination of President Carnot prevented her taking more effective measures than diplomatic representations. In January and February, 1895, when the overwhelming victory of the Japanese forces was obvious to the whole world, Russia began military preparations of some importance. Numerous transports were dispatched from Odessa to the Far East, the survey of the Siberian Railway was ordered to be hurried on, and preparations made for strengthening the Vladivostock squadron.

On February 1st, a circular was sent by the
Russian Foreign Office to the Russian ambassadors
at Paris, London, and elsewhere, outlining the
views of the Czar's government, as to the terms
of peace which Japan should be permitted to
make with China. In the circular it was suggested
that France had already agreed to the Russian
proposals, and that both England and America
would agree to them. This surmise proved to be
painfully incorrect. In the circular it was further
stated that the terms which Japan would be allowed to impose would be limited to the cession
of islands, the imposition of a war indemnity, the
opening of certain ports and trading places, and
the grant of certain commercial concessions, but
under no circumstances would she be allowed to
hold permanently one inch of Chinese territory
on the mainland, though she would be allowed
temporarily to remain in possession of certain
districts, which might be mutually agreed on, to
be held as security for the payment of the indemnity and to be evacuated as the indemnity was
paid off.

Count Hayashi assumes that Germany had had
the intention of intervening from the very beginning of the war, whatever terms of peace might
be made. This assumption does not altogether
appear to be justified. In March, 1895, the German Minister at Tokio had been instructed by
Berlin to warn Japan that any permanent occupation of a portion of the Chinese mainland, as a

condition of peace, would provoke the intervention of Russia. To this Count Hayashi specifically refers. Germany, at the time she gave this warning, was in receipt of the terms of the Russian circular of February 1st, and suspecting that Russia would be only too pleased to take advantage of any incident which might give her the opportunity of interfering and arrogating to herself a decisive position in the Far East, warned Japan in the most friendly spirit. In addition to this Germany, certainly if she had any ambitions herself in the Orient, could not afford not to join Russia and France, after the threat made in July, 1894, that any interference by Russia would result in the Egyptianizing of the Korean question.

In addition there were other motives for Germany joining the Russian protest. Count Caprivi had allowed the "Reassurance Treaty" with Russia to lapse, and that country had made an alliance with France. Since the beginning of the Chino-Japanese War, Prince Hohenlohe had succeeded Count Caprivi as Imperial Chancellor. Hohenlohe was a good deal in touch with Bismarck through his reliance on Count Herbert Bismarck. The early days of the Hohenlohe régime were devoted to trying to regain the Russian position which Caprivi had thrown away, and one of the steps taken towards this end was an almost touching acquiescence in the Russian proposals.

Yet another reason was the Kaiser's personal attitude. It was at this period that he was coming into notice as an earnest advocate of a strong colonial policy and a strong navy. It was on January 9, 1895, that he invited to a soirée at Potsdam all the members of the Reichstag, and delivered to them a vehement lecture on the pressing need of a powerful fleet. As was announced at the time, he worked into this lecture numerous references to the lessons of the war in the Far East. A month later he re-delivered this lecture with further references to the Asiatic situation before the officers of the Marinamt. Then again he demanded more colonies. It is clear that William II. was fully alive to the possibilities of future German development in the Far East, and realized that by having a say in the resettlement of the Treaty of Shimonoseki Germany would be entitled to a voice in all further dealings of Europe with Asia. It certainly does not appear to have ever entered the heads of any of the German statesmen that Japan was a nation whose friendship might one day be of value to Germany. This, however, is not to be wondered at in view of the published opinions of the Kaiser on the coloured races.

There was undoubtedly some sort of agreement between the three Powers as to the price which they were to extract from China for assisting her. According to a Russian statement[1] Russia paid for the co-operation of France with an undertaking

[1] *Novoye Vremya*, April 22, 1895.

to support an eventual French demand for a rectification of the Indo-Chinese frontier, and for Germany's help with a promise to forward German demands for industrial and commercial concessions.

Although the three governments were agreed, the policy of intervention by no means received the unanimous support of the three nations. The German industrial circles were much upset by the commercial privileges obtained by Japan, the Government's reply to an interpellation that the concessions were for all nations being met by the retort that Japan alone could benefit by the 2 per cent. commutation tax on cost, owing to the cheapness of labour in Japan. The German Radicals were loud in their assertion that the transfer of Formosa and the Pescadores to Japan converted the China Sea and the Gulf of Pechili into Japanese lakes. The *Vossische Zeitung* led a very strong campaign against the policy of intervention, arguing that as Germany did not hold a foot of territory in China she had no interest in the business, beyond gratitude to Japan for opening markets which eventually would be of the greatest value to German industries. "In any case," continued the paper, "there is no reason for Germany to strengthen the footing of potential enemies, as Russia and France are, in the Far East."

The *Neueste Nachrichten* of Berlin became curiously prophetic in its disgust at the Government's policy.   It wrote: "In a struggle with France and Russia Japan would be a very useful ally, and her forces are strong enough to distract from her Western frontier a good portion of the Russian armies.   As the end of the affair we seriously fear that Germany will pay bitterly for her action, for the Japanese will eventually seek their revenge."

It is to be hoped that the writer of the above passage is still living, to see the correctness of his deductions.

In France the *Soleil* cleverly expressed the real object of the German Government—to curry favour with the Czar.

The *Figaro* disapproved of the intervention unless Great Britain should agree to join the other Powers.   The journal pointed out that after all Great Britain had the biggest stake in China, and unless she actively acquiesced in the policy of the Triumvirate, she would "open up and monopolize the markets of the Rising Sun, whilst France will be alienated"—another prophecy, which has been almost exactly fulfilled.

Great Britain refused the invitation of Russia to join in the intervention, on the ground that such intervention would be contrary to the established principles of international relationship, and because British interests were in no way menaced. On the contrary, they were considerably benefited by the industrial and commercial concessions extorted from China by Japan for the whole world.   It may be also that public opinion in

England was to some extent sentimentally influenced by the evidence of Japanese progress which the war had afforded, and commercially by a statement from the Japanese Legation that large orders would be forthcoming from Tokio, especially for a new fleet. The refusal of the Russian invitation by Great Britain certainly was of great negative value to the Japanese diplomats. It limited the intervention programme purely to the question of the cession of continental territory and entirely knocked on the head Lobanoff's programme of the retrocession of the Pescadores and the proclamation of a Russian protectorate over Korea.

As the result of the intervention the Mikado's Government withdrew the clause ceding Port Arthur and accepted instead a further indemnity of Tls. 30,000,000, which was raised by a Russian loan to China.

No account of the negotiations which accompanied or followed the signature of the Treaty of Shimonoseki would be complete without noticing a truly Oriental touch in the bargaining on either side. Hayashi points out that both Ito and Mutsu anticipated intervention, and it was only in accordance with the circumstances that they drove a bargain with China from which ample deduction could be made in the event of foreign opposition. Indeed it is not exposing any secret to say that Japan was prepared to retrocede Port Arthur, even without monetary compensa-

tion, and a statement to this effect was actually
and officially issued at Tokio.   Mutsu was strongly
opposed to the Liaotung clause but had to give
way to Ito and the army chiefs.

On the other hand, Li Hung-Chang was equally
astute, and, like Count Witte at Portsmouth,
surrendered nothing which he was not prepared
and glad to get rid of, except the indemnity.   He
always considered Formosa a curse to China, and
was exceedingly pleased to hand it over to Japan,
and he shrewdly guessed that Japan would find
it a great deal more trouble than it was worth.
In this he proved himself a true prophet, for even
to-day (1915) the Japanese have not succeeded in
pacifying Formosa, and insurrections are frequent,
in spite of the drastic methods of the Japanese
gendarmerie.

As regards Liaotung, the Viceroy was more than
willing to sign it away to the Mikado, for he had
already received very definite promises from Count
Cassini that Russia would never permit Japan to
keep it.   Further, he had actually had a proposal
from Russia to lease it herself.   He was only too
delighted to let Japan have the sensation of own-
ing the place as a preliminary to the chagrin of
losing it.   As for the Pescadores they were and
always had been useless to China.   The commercial privileges agreed to were bound to come eventually, as the result of the constant knocking on
the Chinese door by the merchants of Europe and
America.   The permission to import machinery

was merely the translation into law of a custom obtained by bribery.

Li Hung-Chang writes in his *Memoirs* after his return to Pekin from Japan: "I have pored to-day over a mass of translated correspondence from St. Petersburg, part of which is from my friend Count Cassini, and my old frame seems to be given thereby a new elixir of life.

"I can return South with better feelings if less honour.

"Now once more the Throne feels more friendly, but there is an apparent coldness in the treatment accorded me by the Empress. Yet she was gracious enough to acknowledge that the satisfactory assurances are the result of my representations to the Russian Court, last·year, when these troublous times were approaching.

"Briefly we discussed the Russian letters, and their Majesties are heartily grateful that Japan will not be permitted either now or in the future to seize upon any part of Manchuria or the Mainland.

"Why did not I have these assurances before I went to Japan?[1]

"Had I known the way the Czar's Government feels in the matter of Japanese aggressions in Korea and Manchuria, after my armistice proposal had been answered in the manner it was, I could and would have said to Ito, 'Go ahead with the war!'"

[1] He did have them.—ED.

"Still, there is often a very serious doubt in my mind as to the real object of these Europeans, and I have found that some of their most able and honourable diplomats will lie with as much ease as a Nanking bird-hawker."

Again under date of June 11, 1897, he writes: "England has ever asserted that in all my diplomatic work I have had Russia's interests constantly in view. England is very wrong, just as she has been many times before in other matters. If I have appeared to be working for Russia's interest, it is because in doing so I have believed that I was accomplishing the greatest good for China. The British Foreign Office caused me to be rated officially over the Manchurian Agreement with the Czar's Government; but the British refused to say that they would help us in the slightest during our Japanese conflict or after; while Russia, at the close of the war at least, let Japan understand that China was not alone.

"It may not be generally known that as early as 1873, when complaints came from the British traders at Tientsin I earnestly memorialized the Throne to offer Taiwan to the English Government to do with the wretched island as they saw fit." "This memorial," the Viceroy continues, "nearly cost me my position as well as my head. Being summoned to Peking, I was asked by the Grand Council what I meant by advocating that a part of the Imperial territory be given away, to which I replied that it was a hindrance rather

than a benefit to the nation. If the great island
could not be sold I advocated that it be made a
present to England. I told the Council that as
England had been so ready to grab Hong-Kong
we might in a measure get even with her by making
a gift of Formosa.

"It is true that when Marquis Ito made stipulations as one of the chief terms of peace of the
cession of Formosa, I immediately declared that
I was willing to agree to almost anything except
that; yet, had I been in another apartment, all
alone, I would have danced with joy in spite of
my infirmities. As it was, my heart was indeed
glad, but I requested the chief plenipotentiary at
least to say that the Mikado would not insist upon
having the big island. His Excellency agreed to
put the question over until the next session of the
commissioners, and during the intervening time
I was sore afraid that he would change his mind
and make a declaration that his Government did
not want it."[1]

[1] For the above and other details of Li Hung-Chang's negotiations with Marquis Ito and his views on the Treaty the reader
is referred to Mr. Foster's *Memoirs of Li Hung-Chang*.

IV

The Anglo-Japanese Alliance

PROBABLY no diplomatic instrument has been so discussed, so praised, and so abused as the Anglo-Japanese Treaty. Count Hayashi's relation of the preparatory propaganda which he conducted and of the negotiations which preceded its signature is in all likelihood the only authentic account of the intrigues and counter-intrigues of that time which England shall ever have.

The whole of Great Britain's relations with Japan have been so glossed over and so illuminated with a halo that the true condition of affairs in the Far East during the last decade of the nineteenth century has been almost forgotten.

With the exception of a comparatively small circle, Japan, until the Chino-Japanese War, was regarded as being very much of a light-opera country, the setting for dainty music and farcical situations. It was principally thought of as a mysterious land, which was the home of the *musume* and the impressionist painter, where the houses and handkerchiefs were made of paper, where the people wrote with a brush and wore gloves on their feet, worshipped a strange thing called *bushido*, and had a quaint reputation in matters of morality.

The China War changed all this. It was quickly recognized that a new Power had arisen in the East. Many recognized it as a Power potential of great benefits or of great harm. On the whole, there was in England a disposition to treat Japan well. The progress she had shown and the nerve she had displayed created a sentimental feeling in her favour, which was well displayed by Tenniel's cartoons in *Punch*. The Japanese Foreign Office fostered and developed this attitude by the most wonderful Press campaign the world has ever seen.

The very careful manner in which the oracle was worked closed the usual avenues by which a knowledge of the true sentiments, the true policies, and the real intentions of Japan could pass to the outer world.

No man was more intimate with the great statesmen who have shaped the country's destinies than the late Captain Brinkley. Yet, so far as I am aware, it was not until

1904, when he published his monumental work on China and Japan, that he informed the public of the real goal at which the Mikado's Government was aiming. In that book, referring to Japan's object in forcing a war on China, in 1894, he said, "Japan is fighting for the supremacy of the Far East, for the hegemony of Asia. A Japanese proverb says: 'Better be the tail of the ox than the comb of the cock.' By beating China she became the comb of the cock of Asia and will go on to be the tail of the ox."

Old residents in Japan laugh cynically over Japanese asseverations of friendship for England. They recall the days of the war with China, when England was loathed and foreigners were stopped on the streets and asked if they were English, and when the reply was in the affirmative were impolitely told to go to a yet warmer climate. The Japanese equivalent of "Gott strafe England" was a common saying in the streets of Tokio then.

The leaders of Japan have always been divided into two camps. Sometimes they are called the soldiers and the sailors, sometimes Choshu and Satsuma, sometimes anti-British and pro-British.

The military party, the men of Choshu,

are even to-day strongly anti-British, just as the naval party are pro-British. Their dislike of the British is in part an heritage from Ito and the British limitation of the area of the Chinese War, and in part a consequence of their German training and sympathies.

The people, who had no say in the matter, were rather well disposed to England as having held aloof in 1895 and as being their principal customers from whom they expected much future gain.

The following, written by Hitomi Ichitaro in 1897, gives a fair idea of the situation:

"Un peu avant la guerre Chino-Japonaise, l'Angleterre et le Japon se méprisaient l'un l'autre: l'Anglais croyait que la Chine forte et riche était la maîtresse de l'Extrême Orient, et que le Japon pauvre et faible n'était rien.

"Le Cabinet d'Ito a toujours cherché la faveur de la Russie, et affecté de s'éloigner de l'Angleterre: mais le peuple Japonais a méprisé la Russie que le Cabinet craignait et sympathisé avec l'Anglais qu'il repoussait."

The *hakabatsu* (white peril) campaign, the doctrine that the whites are the curse of the yellow race, which was a remarkable accompaniment of the Californian agitation two years ago, was only a revival of a spleen which found an earlier but not less violent

expression eighteen years before and was led
on both occasions by Tokutomi, Okuma, and
the Choshu clan.

So far as Japan is concerned, any alliance
between herself and a white race must be one
of political expediency. There can be no
other ground or justification for it. The
Japanese are Orientals. It is perfectly futile
to argue that their veneer of Western civilization has made them anything else. If the
Chinese and Japanese have a vicious deep-
seated contempt for each other, as they have,
it is nothing in comparison with the innate
contempt, the burning detestation, which the
Japanese have *in excelsis* for all white men.

Since 1895 this feeling has been deliberately
educated and developed by the Japanese
authorities, by means of that most extraordinary religion which Professor Basil Chamberlain has so ably and relentlessly exposed,
namely, Mikado-worship.[1]

The idea was sown and fostered and has
grown into a national creed, that there is no
country in the world which is so great as
Japan, and that any and every other country
is infinitely inferior. This idea has found
utterance on numerous occasions in official

[1] *The Making of a New Religion.* By Prof. B. Chamberlain.
London, 1911.

5

documents and in the Diet, both from the lips of Ministers and members. One expression of it, which is worth remembering in these days of land agitation in California and British Columbia, is the refusal to allow foreigners to own land, because such ownership would be a "pollution of the sacred soil."

In all matters concerning Japan it has to be remembered that public opinion in that country is practically non-existent, except on such rare occasions as after the Treaties of Shimonoseki and Portsmouth and at the death of the Meiji Tenno, when the sentiment of the whole people was deeply affected. The political riots which are now almost an annual feature of life in Tokio are not expressions of public opinion but the carefully organized demonstrations of the "outs" against the "ins."

It is for this reason that the Alliance was and is, so far as Japan is concerned, a political expedient. I believe that the Japanese people themselves would at one time, if they had been canvassed and allowed to vote freely (which would have been a rarity for them), have been found to appreciate it deeply. But this would not have been for any reasons of foreign policy, but because the Japanese people are a folk trying to be politically free

and to attain, themselves, to those heights
of democracy at which they know England
has already arrived. The time for that is,
however, past. The Alliance now means to
them nothing but an increase of expenditure,
a constant rise in taxes, and a constant soaring
of the cost of living.

The great development of reading the
numerous translations of American and English works, is gradually arousing a general
feeling that the country must be governed by
the people for the people. The consistent
disregard for the rights of the individual shown
by such men as Prince Yamagata, the late
Prince Katsura, Viscount Oura, and Count
Okuma, the steadily mounting debt and the
increasing burden of taxation, are creating a
social unrest that must before long find an
escape. In Japan all that is required for a
popular outbreak on a scale with which Imperial edicts and Ministerial platitudes will be
unable to cope is a leader who will prove himself worthy of public confidence and adamant
against bribes of office and reward.

When that day comes it will be a duty of
the British Government to show that the
Alliance, if still in force, is not only a diplomatic instrument to secure Japan's military
aid in time of crisis, but is also founded on a

sincere regard for the Japanese people themselves and a desire to see them develop along the true lines of Western civilization and freedom.

At the present time the Alliance is merely a political arrangement between governments, which is used by the Japanese bureaucrats as an excuse, and a very plausible one, for constant additions to armaments, and as a safeguard for themselves in a policy of aggression and expansion, which has for its ultimate object a protectorate over China.

Whether from the English point of view the Alliance has attained the objects intended is a matter of doubt! Whether it was ever really necessary or advisable is a frequent subject of discussion!

When the first alliance was signed its honest *ultima ratio,* so far as England was concerned, was fear of Russian aggression on India and Constantinople. So far as Japan was concerned it was the absorption of Korea and a predominating position in China. England was to keep the ring whilst Japan attacked Russia.

The net result was that Russia's ambitions on the Pacific were checked and diverted to Persia, Central Asia, and the Balkans, where she is considerably nearer to India and her manifest destiny, Constantinople, than ever before. The document which provided for the integrity of China and the independence of Korea handed over the latter country for annexation by Japan, and a slice of the Chinese Empire as big as India to Japanese control. A British Government which had put its seal to the Alliance, ostensibly to ensure China's sovereignty over her own territories, became an active party to the abrogation of that sovereignty over a vast stretch of China. It is not, perhaps, to be wondered at that Germany expressed surprise at England's respect for a "scrap of paper" in August of last year.

The second alliance treaty was the reiteration of the first on a broader basis, except that Germany was the enemy feared, and that it included the enunciation of Japan's reward for her services against Russia.

The third alliance treaty was an emasculation of the second by the removal of any possibility of England's being called on to fight America. It has been a source of the greatest dissatisfaction in Japan, for America is the one Power which Japan fears may attempt to annul her claims to keep China in leading strings.

It will be for the historian to decide to what extent any of these treaties were necessary, and how far they were due to a lack of political foresight. The ostensible cause of the first treaty, namely the integrity and independence of Korea, was of course nonsense. Lord Lansdowne declared England had no important interests in Korea. Then why did he mix England up in the affairs of the Hermit Kingdom? Why did he sign a treaty which he gravely feared was one-sided?

The British Government was repeatedly warned in 1895 that Japan and Russia must one day fight about Korea. England had nothing to gain by interference. By being inveigled into the arena she has lost the whole of her interests in Korea, Manchuria, Shantung, and Fukien, and much of her prestige in China.

Count Hayashi reveals two things of great importance. The first that Count Witte in 1897 and 1898 proposed a *rapprochement* with England, which failed on account of the attitude of the Press and the city. It would be interesting to know to what extent Japan influenced that attitude.

Secondly, he says Germany proposed a Triple Alliance of Britain, Germany, and Japan, from which Germany was eventually cold-shouldered.[1] Attempts have been made

---

[1] This statement has been denied in Berlin. On the other hand, I have heard it confirmed by German diplomats of high rank.

in interested quarters to minimize the importance of this statement.   It cannot be mini-
mized.   It is the key to everything that has
happened since in the Far East, and of much
that has happened in Europe.   This exclusion
in 1902 was the first of a long series of similar
acts, each and every one of which was intended
to shut Germany out of the Far East.   It
will be an important duty of the historians
of posterity to decide to what extent German
ambitions have been clipped and German
opposition to England developed by the
manner of her treatment in the East of Asia.
The political idealist can find food for thought
at what would have happened if either of
these overtures had materialized, and then
consign his vain reflections to the limbo of
diplomatic might-have-beens.

The only justification of the Anglo-Japanese
Alliance is that *existence* in Europe outweighs *interests* in Asia.   It will be for Time, the inexora-
ble accountant, to decide to what extent the
menace to England's existence in Europe was
due to slovenly diplomacy, and to what extent the sacrifices England has made in Asia
have been recompensed in the moment of trial.

China is the country which has most reason
to complain of England's policy in the Far East.
Instead of the Alliance really safeguarding

her rights and territory, the process of absorption and the policy of aggression by neighbouring Powers had been vastly accelerated since 1902. As the *Sinwan Pao* expressed it this year: "If the value of the Alliance is only to substitute a lingering death for a quick one, then so far as China is concerned it has no value at all. Beheading is infinitely preferable to the thousand slices." That Japan has been the most wanton aggressor is now generally recognized. But that she has been in a position to carry out successfully such a policy is due to the Alliance of 1902 and its corollaries.

I shall be very much surprised if within a few years England does not realize that her money and her support have raised up against us in the Far East a Power as powerful and as dangerous as Germany has become, and one infinitely more difficult to handle on account of her geographical position.

Japan is distinctly a country to be treated with cautious courtesy and a country about which English statesmen require to know a great deal more than they do know. A theocratic bureaucracy is probably the most effective government conceivable. Obedience is its watchword. In Japan the world has the most highly organized bureaucratic machine in existence. As ex-President Roosevelt would put it, "They have Germany beat to a frazzle."

It must be remembered, too, that the Japanese are first-class diplomats, and everything which that connotes. In Oriental diplomacy there is no room for scruples.

Diplomacy is war in the council chamber instead of on the field. The true diplomat combines the subtlety of the serpent with the simplicity of the dove. He may affect to believe everything and should, in fact, believe nothing. He has his goal marked out and has to get there or as near to it as may be humanly possible. In Japan the European diplomat lives in an atmosphere of blandishment and *bushido*, but he should never forget that the "ethics of bushido make no distinction between the 'ways which are dark and the tricks which are vain' so long as the aim is attained." Hence I may say again that England's policy in the Far East should be one of polite preparation.

If a study of the late Count Hayashi's *Memoirs* in the light of subsequent events opens the eyes of the public to the futility of a foreign policy which looks only to immediate gain and recklessly disregards the future, then they will not have failed in the purpose of their publication.

A. M. P.

THE SECRET MEMOIRS OF
COUNT HAYASHI

CHAPTER I

Origin of an Opinion for an Anglo-Japanese Alliance

THE origin of the desire for an alliance to be concluded between Great Britain and Japan is to be traced to the feeling existent in political circles in the latter country after the close of the Chino-Japanese War, when the intervention of the three Powers, Russia, France, and Germany, necessitated the retrocession of Port Arthur.

Prior to that intervention and during the progress of the war with China, France had shown herself to be friendly to Japan, a feeling which was reciprocated by that country.

As regards the relations between Great Britain and Japan, the late Count Ito, who was at that time the President of the Council of Ministers, before the war with China was decided on, entertained great anxiety as to the real position which Great Britain would take up. His anxiety was shared by other persons occupying important positions in the State and at Court. They feared lest Great Britain might have a secret agreement with China, and in the event of war breaking out with Japan, she might render China some aid.

Although Great Britain had tried very hard to prevent the outbreak of hostilities between Japan and China, when it was certain that nothing could hinder such a development instructions were given to the British Chargé d'Affaires at Tokio at the end of July, 1894, to demand from Japan a guarantee that Shanghai and its vicinity should be regarded as outside the area of hostilities.

As a result of this demand from the side of the British Government, the Japanese authorities realized that Great Britain had no secret agreement with China, and in consequence war with China was resolved upon on August 1, 1894.

An important matter at this time was that the negotiations for the revision of the Anglo-Japanese Commercial Treaty had been concluded, and shortly before the declaration of war Great Britain had requested an early exchange of ratifications. This appeared to signify that, victory or defeat, neither result would affect the question of the revision of the treaty.

The net result of this was that Great Britain's attitude proved in reality to be the exact opposite of what the Japanese authorities believed it was. Instead of being bound to China and hostile to Japan, Great Britain seemed favourably inclined to the latter country. On the other hand, the interference of the three continental Powers after the conclusion of the war seriously affecting the interests of Japan had the result of drawing Japan towards Great Britain, and created an opinion very favourable towards a future Anglo-Japanese Alliance.

The Three-Power Intervention, 1895.

The first hint of the possibility of interference with the policy of Japan in connexion with the conditions to be imposed by her on China as the result of her victories came from the dispatches sent to the London *Times* by its famous correspondent at Paris, M. de Blowitz, during January and February, 1895. Both the Premier, Count Ito, and the Foreign Minister, M. Mutsu, anticipated such action on the part of Russia, France, and Germany, but they were quite unable to anticipate what direction intervention would take, nor could they guess to what extent it would be carried. They considered the matter and came to the conclusion that even if they were to make less stringent terms with China than those which they had in view, it would still be impossible to avoid intervention from the side of the Powers, as it was quite certain that the latter had made up their minds to control China's action and also to deal a deadly blow at Japan.

Consequently the Japanese statesmen determined to make no alteration in the terms of peace which they already had in mind, but to go as far as possible without paying any immediate attention to the prospect of intervention by the continental Powers.

Of course it was quite clear that intervention from the side of Russia would mean an excellent opportunity for that country to extend her influence in the Far East, and it was very natural that she was at the bottom of the whole affair. France had an Alliance with Russia and on account of that Alliance was obliged to support Russia's action, in spite of her own earlier friendship for Japan. The statement of M. Harmand, the French Minister to Tokio at the time, fully proved the real circumstances actuating French policy.

As for Germany, she had no reason whatsoever for being at enmity with Japan, and
she had no obligation whatsoever in Europe
to oblige her to support Russia, as was the
case with France. On the occasion of the
signature of the Treaty of Shimonoseki,
which concluded the war between China and
Japan, the German Minister at Tokio, Baron
von Gutschmid, was the first to dispatch a
telegram of congratulation to the Foreign
Minister. Consequently it was a great surprise to the Japanese when Germany suddenly
changed her attitude and agreed to take
common action with France and Russia, to
obtain the surrender of Port Arthur by us.

An inquiry was made by our Foreign Office
from the German Minister in Tokio as to
the reason for German action in joining Russia
and France. Baron von Gutschmid replied
very composedly that the German Government had given warning to the Japanese
Government at the beginning of 1895, and
had at that time pointed out that intervention
by the Powers would be inevitable if Japan
should take any steps towards the partition
of Manchuria. In spite of this friendly warning the Japanese Government had concluded
a treaty with China embodying territorial
acquisition, and as a consequence Germany

6

was forced to stand by the side of Russia and France.

This must indeed be called a strange explanation. Preliminary notice as to the possibility of intervention might possibly be listened to, but that a country should join in intervention, simply because of non-acceptance of the warning, is to me incomprehensible.

In short, it must be assumed that Russia and France intervened solely on account of our territorial aggrandizement, but Germany had had the intention of intervening, whatever conditions of peace were made, long before the conclusion of the treaty of peace.

With regard to the attitude of the German Government towards Japan at the time of the intervention, the following interesting anecdote throws some light.

At the time of the intervention of the three Powers, Count Mutsu, the Foreign Minister, was absent in the Kyoto district, and the management of the Ministry of Foreign Affairs was in my hands, and it was I who carried on the negotiations with the Ministers of the three Powers. On one occasion (April 23, 1895) the Russian and French Ministers called on me at the Foreign Office and brought and read to me a memorandum briefly written in the French language and left it for my further perusal and consideration.

The same day the German Minister called, but later in the afternoon. In spite of a sufficient knowledge of English and French, the German Minister apparently thought it an indignity to draft a memorandum in either of these languages, and in consequence of my inability to understand German brought me a memorandum written in *romaji* (Japanese written in Roman letters, according to the Japanese phonetics), and caused his secretary, Herr Weipert, to read it out. Now the secretary was extremely well acquainted with the ordinary Japanese script and was vexed at having to read out an unfamiliar transcript of the original text, which had been composed from Chinese ideographs. It was quite clear that neither the secretary nor the Minister understood a single word of what the former was reading, whilst I, though paying the deepest attention, was barely able to catch the meaning of the memorandum.

The memorandum which had been left by the French and Russian Ministers was practically a brief sentence advising the retrocession of the territory acquired by the Treaty of Shimonoseki, and giving as a reason for the advice friendship for the neighbouring country.

The German memorandum, on the other hand, said that there was no possibility of Japan being able to hope for a victory in fighting Russia, Germany, and France, and therefore it would be beneficial for Japan if the advice tendered by the three Powers should be accepted.

Standing at the table opposite to the German Minister I said, "Your Excellency's colleagues, the Ministers of Russia and France, have been here and have given friendly advice for the purpose of maintaining peace, and in doing so they have used a friendly terminology. But your Excellency's memorandum is phrased as if it were the proposal to solve the question by force of arms. If you mean this then the dignity of the State, as well as the feeling of the nation, must be considered, let alone the words in which the memorandum is couched. It seems as if the memorandum has been written in the Japanese language, with which you are unfamiliar, and consequently errors have been made in the use of words."

The German Minister, in the most awkward manner, said that the views expressed by me as being in the memorandum were not so meant, and if such views occurred in it, it was due to errors in the wording of the memorandum in Japanese. He promised to cancel the memorandum and asked me to regard the German memorandum as being identical with those of the Russian and French Ministers.

NOTE. The following was the text of the Russian Note, which was also adopted by the French Minister, and, in the circumstances described above, by the German Minister, with, of course, the necessary verbal alterations.

"The Government of His Majesty the Emperor of All the Russias, in examining the conditions of peace which Japan has imposed on China, finds that the possession of the Peninsula of Liaotung, claimed by Japan, would be a constant menace to the capital of China, would at the same time render illusory the independence of Korea, and would henceforth be a perpetual obstacle to the peace of the Far East.

"Consequently the Government of His Majesty the Emperor would give a new proof of their sincere friendship for the Government of His Majesty the Emperor of Japan by advising them to renounce the definite possession of the Peninsula of Liaotung."—ED.

CHAPTER II

Preliminaries of the Alliance

As the result of the intervention by the three Powers after the Treaty of Shimonoseki, the interests of the different countries in the Far East fell into a new grouping. France and Germany stood with Russia on the one side; whilst Great Britain, Japan, and the United States stood on the other. The result of this was that an opinion gradually spread both amongst the public and in the official world at Tokio that an alliance with Great Britain would be beneficial.

The Alliance was really an epoch-making event, when it had been concluded. It stands out in the history of the world. The glorious victories of our army and navy in the Russo-Japanese War and the great fight in the Straits of Tsushima were in themselves almost unprecedented in the history of warfare, but they could never have taken place without the Anglo-Japanese Alliance.

After the war great changes took place in the relations between the Powers. Those Powers which had previously been antipathetic to Japan arranged compromises, and now there is no reason to anticipate another war. This result has been due entirely to the virtue of the alliance.

Not one of the persons who, after the retrocession of Port Arthur, approved the idea of an alliance, ever imagined that it would have such far-reaching consequences. They only felt at the time of discussing it that without some sort of support the pressure of the European Powers might be renewed. Indeed, there were even different opinions as to whether an alliance with Great Britain would be the most suitable for our requirements, or whether a Russo-Japanese Alliance or even a Russo-Franco-Japanese Alliance would not be better. Both these latter proposals received the support of minorities in Japan. The main point kept in view by everybody was, however, that Japan's isolated position must be abandoned.

I admit that I felt most strongly the attitude of Germany in the intervention question, as I considered that that country had no interest whatsoever in the matter. On the other hand, I keenly appreciated the joint interests of Russia and France, with the result that shortly after the intervention question had been settled I wrote an essay bearing the title: "Future Policy in Foreign Affairs." This was completed towards the end of May, 1895, and I presented it to the late Mr. Fukuzawa, the proprietor and managing editor of the *Jiji Shimpo*. This gentleman was a great *savant*, and entirely agreed with the views expressed therein, with the result that in June, 1895, he published the essay in the *Jiji Shimpo*. Shortly afterwards I was appointed Minister to China and left Tokio for Peking. A few days after my departure, on June 21st, the *Jiji Shimpo* published yet another article from my pen, again setting out my views on the country's foreign policy and emphasizing the necessity for the conclusion of some sort of an arrangement with Great Britain. The considerable attention paid to these two articles by the general public is evidence enough that the idea of an alliance was beginning to obtain a hold amongst the people.

The then Foreign Minister, Count Mutsu (created Count after the Treaty with China), was also in favour of an alliance.

During the whole of my residence in Peking, and later in St. Petersburg, having the object of creating the alliance always in view, I tried continuously to cultivate the society of the British representatives at those places. I therefore considered it a matter for self-congratulation that Sir Nicholas O'Connor, who had been my colleague in Peking, should also have been my colleague in St. Petersburg.

The idea of the alliance gradually extended until, on a certain day in March, 1898, Mr. Joseph Chamberlain, the then Minister for the Colonies in the English Cabinet, had a conversation with M. (later Baron) Kato, who at the time was the Japanese Minister in London, at a public banquet, which both were attending. Mr. Chamberlain on that occasion expressed to M. Kato the readiness of Great Britain to enter into an agreement with Japan for the settlement of relations in the Far East. M. Kato sent a long telegram to Count Okuma, at that time the Minister for Foreign Affairs at Tokio, and urged on him the advisability of complying with the British statesman's wishes.[1]

In 1899 I returned to Tokio from St.

---

[1] Kato, Taka-aki, b. 1859. Entered Foreign Office, 1887; Private Secretary to Foreign Minister, Count Okuma, 1888; Minister at London, 1894–99; Ambassador at London, 1906–13; Minister for Foreign Affairs, 1900–01, 1906, 1913, 1914; G.C.M.G.

Okuma, Shigenobu, b. 1838. Foreign Minister, 1888, 1896–97; 1898–99; Premier, 1897, 1914.—ED.

Petersburg and visited Count Ito at his residence on Reinanzaka (one of the residential quarters in Tokio). Count Inouye was present at that interview, and asked me if I would like to go to London as Minister. To this inquiry I replied that such was my most earnest desire.

Count Inouye then continued by saying that M. Kato was always pressing on the Foreign Office the urgent necessity of an alliance with Great Britain, and he asked for my views on the matter. I replied that I considered the alliance to be most advisable and important, but pointed out that an alliance means something mutual, each side bringing something into the bargain. If Japan were not able to bring sufficient into the alliance as her contribution then indeed it might suit Great Britain better to make an arrangement with Russia, which country could certainly offer more than Japan. And even if matters should not go so far as an Anglo-Russian Alliance, it might well be that the idea of an Anglo-Japanese Alliance would be blocked. I said that my experience in Russia had been that England was very popular with certain sections, and therefore it would be very difficult to bring about an Anglo-Japanese Alliance. To explain this statement I then added certain particulars of matters which had happened whilst I was Minister in St. Petersburg (March, 1897–1899).

Pourparlers that miscarried.

At the time when I was Minister at St. Petersburg the Russian Government was getting more and more interested in Far Eastern affairs.

It is digressing a little to relate the following story, but as it concerned a very important matter and was illustrative of the above I will "strike it in, whilst the iron is hot." In regard to the Korean question in 1897, in disregard of the Yamagata-Lobanoff Agreement,[1] the Russian Government, without

---

[1] The Yamagata-Lobanoff Agreement was signed at St. Petersburg in 1896 on the occasion of the visit of Field-Marshal Count (now Prince) Yamagata to St. Petersburg to represent the Mikado on the occasion of the coronation of the Tsar and Tsarina. The agreement was to all intents and purposes merely a ratification of the Komura-Waeber Convention, signed at Seoul on May 13, 1896, by the late M. (afterwards Marquis) Jutaro Komura, then Japanese Minister to Korea, and M. G. Waeber, Russian Minister to Korea. Under the Komura-Waeber Convention both Powers obtained the right to maintain a Legation guard of 800 men, whilst Japan obtained the further right to maintain a telegraph guard of 200 men to patrol the cable line between Fusan and Seoul, which was the property of a Japanese concessionaire.—Ed.

notifying the Japanese Government, sent several military officers to Korea for the purpose of training the Korean army, and also a financial adviser. Count Okuma, who was then the Minister of Foreign Affairs at Tokio, protested against this to the Russian Government, and I, in accordance with his instructions, saw Count Muravieff on the matter. He said to me, "That is something which happened under my predecessor, and I have nothing to do with it." I replied that a Government's responsibility could not change just because the Foreign Minister changed. "Well," he said, "to tell you the truth the Korean Emperor desired to have some military advisers, and so we sent them. We could not refuse the request of the ruler of a country with whom we have (diplomatic) relations."

I then asked: "Would you then comply with any request made to you by the Emperor of Korea? Would you act thus in defiance of the convention which you have signed with us? If so, the agreement you have made with Japan is not worth the paper on which it is written. I must ask you to let us know exactly where we stand." "No," replied Count Muravieff. "What I mean is that we have sent these officers to Korea and we cannot recall them immediately. As a matter of fact, we were to have increased their numbers, but we will not send any more. We will correct the matter and make amends to you for it as you consider it a violation of the agreement. But we must have some further time for the matter to be settled in." This ended the conversation, but there was never any definite settlement of the matter.

Meanwhile there had been a change of Ministry at Tokio, and the third Ito Cabinet had taken office with Baron Nishi as Foreign Minister.

In January, 1898, the Russian Foreign Minister proposed, acting under the direct instructions of the Tsar, to negotiate an agreement with Japan in regard to Korea. I at once telegraphed this information to Tokio, and as our Government also wanted to have the question settled I received telegraphic instructions to agree.

The Nishi-Rosen Negotiations.

My own opinion was that if Japan and Russia were to make an agreement that should require both countries to retire from Korea, then Japan's interests being so complicated she might be obliged to have to stand by, only being able to watch whatever might occur internally in Korea. (It should be remembered that, since the China War, Japan had very materially increased her interests in Korea, independently of her political situation toward that country. At the close of 1897, for example, she obtained the concession for the Seoul-Fusan Railway.) Russia having fewer interests internally in Korea might also be content to stand by and watch, but, on the other hand, might, in spite of the agreement, interfere if anything serious should happen. It appeared to me therefore better for both countries to be able to send advisers to Korea, a course which, as I thought, might work out more advantageously than any agreement on the other lines proposed at the time could do.

There were already a number of Russian military advisers in Korea training the Korean army, and as their number was large it would be a difficult matter to recall them. There was also one financial adviser, M. Alexeieff (head of the short-lived Russo-Korean Bank. He succeeded Mr. McLeavy Brown as Financial Adviser to Korea in the autumn of 1897). His recall would not, however, be a difficult matter. I thought that Japan should prefer to supply Korea with a financial adviser, rather than with military advisers. I therefore telegraphed to Tokio suggesting that a clause might be inserted in the proposed agreement, that Russia and Japan should mutually agree to take over the military and financial adviserships respectively. Later, the negotiations were transferred to Tokio and in April, 1898, the Nishi-Rosen Convention was signed, whereunder military and financial advisers to Korea should only be appointed with the mutual consent of both countries.[1]

Whilst the negotiations for this convention were in progress it looked as though the question of the appointment of the military and financial advisers to Korea might create some trouble.

Russian Clumsiness.

Just at that time the Russian Government presented certain demands to the Korean Government. The Korean authorities were as usual very dilatory in their reply. M. Spiers, the Russian Chargé d'Affaires, de-

[1] The Nishi-Rosen Convention stated that both countries recognized the sovereignty and entire independence of Korea and pledged themselves not to interfere in the internal affairs of Korea. Russia agreed not to interfere with the development of the commercial and industrial relations between Korea and Japan, and neither country should send advisers to Korea without the consent of the other party to the Convention.—ED.

manded a reply within a certain definite time, and threatened if a reply were not forthcoming within the time limit to withdraw the Russian military and financial advisers. The Korean monarch was very frightened and confidentially asked the Japanese Minister, M. Kato, for his advice. M. Kato gave him the following opinion: "Since the Russians threaten to withdraw their advisers on their own account, it would be perfectly correct for you to consent to the withdrawal, unless—you are anxious to retain their services!"

The Korean Government at once informed the Russian representative that Korea had no need of the services of the Russian advisers and consequently he could order their withdrawal as soon as he liked. The Russian representative was hoist with his own petard. He could not very well eat his words. He therefore thundered at the Korean Ministers: "If you think that you can take care of yourselves, just remember not to get any more foreign advisers to come and help you." He then flung out and sent the Russian officers home.[1]

[1] When the Convention had been signed the Russo-Korean Bank put up its shutters, and M. Alexeieff followed his military colleagues home. Col. Potiola and the Legation guard followed shortly after.—Ed.

The precipitate action of the Russian Chargé thus solved the difficulty which lay in the way of the conclusion of the Convention, for the advisers having disappeared it was possible to arrange that no others should be sent without mutual consent. Later, when I met the Russian Foreign Minister, he said to me: "We have recalled the military officers whom we had sent to Korea. I hope that you are now satisfied!" I replied, "I certainly should be satisfied, but since you have withdrawn them of your own accord, there is no special reason for Japan to thank you."

Who intervened first?

As I have digressed so far from my main theme I may as well digress a little further to mention another matter which occurred about the same time as those events which I have just been discussing. I refer to the leasing of Port Arthur.

The Yin-chow (Liaotung) Peninsula had once been Japanese territory, under the terms of the Treaty of Shimonoseki. On account of the intervention by the three Powers, Russia, France, and Germany, we restored it to China, receiving in return an indemnity of Tls. 30,000,000. China raised the loans to furnish this and the war indemnity on guarantees given by Russia. In payment for this service China agreed to give Russia a concession for a branch of the Siberian Railway, which was to penetrate Northern Manchuria. Each one of these steps had been planned by Count Witte, the Russian Minister of Finance.

At that time there was living in Paris a certain M. Schion, who had formerly been a Councillor in the Department of Finance at St. Petersburg. He had resigned his post on account of disagreements with the policy of Count Witte, and from his retirement at Paris published open letters attacking very trenchantly the policy of his former chief. These attacks were the more serious inasmuch as they were based on material which he had collected when employed at the finance department. Amongst other things exposed by M. Schion was the fact that it was Count Witte who had initiated the policy of intervention at the conclusion of the Chino-Japanese War, and further, that he was prepared to carry that policy to the point of hostilities, if necessary. Indeed (according to M. Schion), Count Witte had given Count Lobanoff, the then Russian Foreign Minister, assurances that he would guarantee the raising of sufficient funds to carry on war, if it should become necessary.

Later I heard from my British colleague at St. Petersburg, Sir Nicholas O'Connor, that Count Lobanoff had once assured him that Count Witte was entirely responsible for the intervention and retrocession policy, and that he, Count Lobanoff, had only been entrusted with the execution of the programme drawn up by the Finance Minister. I am therefore inclined to believe that M. Schion was writing the truth in his open letters.

Count Witte's Programme.

M. Schion went even further, however. He attacked the scheme for the penetration of Northern Manchuria with a railway. He pointed out that as part of it would run through the territory of another nation it would be very difficult for Russia to defend that portion of the line. Again, he wrote that the primary objects of a railway should not be only to connect the termini of the line but also to tap the regions through which it should pass. The value of a line could not be estimated simply by its mileage track.

In my opinion, however, M. Schion's argument on this point is fallacious, because

Count Witte never had any intention of respecting China's sovereignty over the portion of Chinese territory through which the railway would pass.

Count Witte's programme was to build a railway, to create cities along that railway, to develop the regions through which it passed, and, as soon as this had been effected in the Sungari district, to move on down to the south. By this means the gradual development of the line would blind other nations, and by the time the crisis in the Far East should arrive, Russian power would be so fully developed and so strong that no other country would or could dare to risk opposing her advance.

Moreover, by this method Count Witte would have been able to effect considerable financial economies in the construction of the line, for each section of it would have been self-supporting.

The diplomacy by which the Count created the Triple Entente for the purpose of intimidating Japan had been very striking. The Count did not speak any English, and so I was never able to talk intimately with him, although I met him often. Nevertheless I could not do otherwise than admire his ability as a statesman. Had his programme been carried out as he at first proposed, what would not have been the result? But just after the programme had been planned an event took place which ate up an enormous amount of money. This was the leasing of Port Arthur.

The Occupation of Kiaochow.

However, before I speak of the Russian occupation of Port Arthur I shall discuss the German occupation of Kiaochow.

As a recompense for the support rendered by the Triple Entente to China, Russia obtained the concession for the construction of the Chinese Eastern Railway (August 27th, September 8, 1896), France obtained concessions in Yunnan and along the Yangtse, but Germany only obtained the concession of a portion of the city of Tientsin for the exclusive use of the German colony at that place. This was not enough for Germany. She naturally yearned after a concession at Kiaochow. [1]

[1] Kiaochow, according to the reputed Cassini Convention, had been earmarked by Russia. The premature publication of this famous document by the *North China Daily News* in August, 1896, gave the Far East such a shock that both China and Russia vehemently denied the authenticity of the document. The Chinese Eastern Railway Agreement is, however, so obvi-

How Germany managed to obtain her enormous interests in Shantung, everybody knows![1]

When Germany first secured the concession of Kiaochow, she had no idea why she wanted it. She took it haphazard, without any definite end in view. This is seen by the

ously framed on the Cassini Convention that the denial has not gained much credence. There is reason to believe that the Cassini Convention was a draft agreement intended to bind China down on the Manchurian question, but not intended to be ratified or promulgated.—Ed.

[1] The Kiaochow Concession was extorted from China as indemnity for the murder of two German missionaries in Shantung in the autumn of 1897. Kiaochow was seized on November 14, 1897, pending the settlement of the diplomatic questions raised. In order to make the weight of the mailed fist still more impressive, Baron von Heyking, the German Minister at Peking, was ordered to prolong the negotiations by refusing to accept any offers of reparation made by China. Meanwhile Prince Henry of Prussia was dispatched to the Far East at the head of a strong squadron. On March 6, 1898, the leasing agreement was signed. Tsingtao, which is the official German name of the colony, has proved itself a white elephant to the German Government, a destiny which was perhaps expected in view of the retrocession clause contained in the agreement. In 1914, on the outbreak of the war between the Triple Entente and Japan, and Germany and Austria, in response to the request of the British Government that Japan should put into force the terms of the Anglo-Japanese Alliance, the Mikado's Government sent an ultimatum to Berlin demanding the unconditional surrender of Tsingtao to Japan for eventual retrocession to China. The demand being unanswered, siege operations were undertaken by a combined British and Japanese naval and military force and the fortress surrendered in November, 1914. At the time of writing it has not yet been restored to China.—Ed.

fifth clause of the lease which provides that in the case Germany should desire to vacate the concession before the expiration of the lease, China shall refund to her any money expended on the same, and also shall grant to Germany a more appropriate territory.

At the time of the Kiaochow affair, acting under instructions from the Foreign Office at Tokio, I called on the Russian Foreign Minister, and asked him for his opinion as to Germany's true intentions. Count Muravieff replied: "Probably the Kaiser wanted it in order to encourage the expansion of the German Navy." I then asked him: "Was your Government consulted about it?" He replied: "No, we were not. We were only informed of the matter after the place had been seized."

However, the very month after the Kiaochow lease was signed the lease of Port Arthur to Russia was signed (March 27– April 9, 1898). I cannot help thinking, therefore, that there was a secret agreement between Germany and Russia on the matter, in spite of Count Muravieff's statement to me.

In that case the negotiations with Japan on the Korean question at about that time were only intended to blind that country as to Russia's true intentions on the mainland.[1]

What crippled Russia afterwards was the useless expenditure of enormous sums of money immediately after her acquisition of Port Arthur, and with no prospect of getting any returns. Having obtained that place she at once wanted to occupy Manchuria. As the proverb says, "The hunter who chases

[1] Count Hayashi's assumption does not appear to be justified. Not only did both Count Witte and the Russian Foreign Minister explicitly deny at the time that there was any previous arrangement with Germany, but as Count Hayashi has earlier pointed out, the acquisition of Port Arthur at that moment was rather an unfortunate event for Russia, as it upset Count Witte's railway schemes. Probably the Russian statesmen considered that this inconvenience must be endured for reasons of strategy and prestige. In addition to these presumptions there is more direct evidence on the point. After the Boxer Rebellion the secret archives of the Tsung-li-yamen fell into foreign hands, and completely established the statement that Russia instructed her representative at Peking to do everything possible to block the granting of the lease to Germany. In Europe also everything was done to try to turn the Kaiser from his objective, as Russia had always considered Kiaochow earmarked for an ice-free base for her Pacific fleet. To Prince Henry of Prussia is owing the information of how the deadlock was terminated. In a speech before the German club at Shanghai he told how the Kaiser had met the Tsar, and pointed out that Germany was in Kiaochow and intended to stop there. Russia could have no claim to the place, because the Cassini Convention, which was the only document mentioning it, had been declared by both Russia and China to be spurious. He suggested that Russia should take Port Arthur and Talienwan, which would be far more suitable to her needs, as they could be made into great military outposts, and Russia's future in the Far East was obviously on the mainland.—ED.

the deer does not see the mountain before him." Russia plunged into the absorption of Manchuria without regard to the opinions of other countries, and this policy led her to the war with Japan.

Rivalry for Power.

There is no clear evidence to prove it, but there appears to have been something behind the leasing of Port Arthur. Count Witte and Count Muravieff were really rivals for power. Each wanted to do something which would hand his name down to posterity as famous. It was this which led to the leasing of Port Arthur. Judging from the statements current in Russian political circles at that time, there was a good deal of truth in this story of rivalry between the two statesmen.

About that time I met Count Muravieff accidentally. He said to me: "The agreement for the lease of Port Arthur has been signed. As, however, events have moved so rapidly we have no map of that region. Now as Japan once held Port Arthur it is probable that you have a good map of that territory. If this is so, would you be so kind as to lend it to me?" I smiled as I looked at the Count, and I replied: "Certainly Port Arthur was once occupied by Japan, and we have very good maps of that region. But we have none of them in our Legation here. And even if we had I could not comply with your request, though if I can accommodate you in any other way I would be glad to do so." The Count smiled grimly and said: "You are quite right and I don't blame you."

The intervention of the three Powers had taken place under his predecessor, and he did not at the moment remember it. Anyhow, the leasing of Port Arthur had taken place so hurriedly that he had no maps of the district and had come to me to borrow one!

Sometime after when negotiating with the British Minister the Count mixed up Dairen (Dalny) and Port Arthur, and there was a bitter quarrel between them, as a result of which the British Minister was transferred to Turkey. But the cause was most certainly Count Muravieff's extraordinary lack of geographical knowledge.

Russia's pro-British Policy.

After the lease of Port Arthur, Counts Witte and Muravieff became estranged. The latter was the protégé of the Empress Dowager Marie (he was also the son of Muravieff of

Amur fame), and had been promoted to be
Minister of Foreign Affairs from the very insignificant post of Minister to Denmark. He
had therefore considerable influence with the
Tsar and the Court. His Far Eastern policies
were very well conceived and executed. Now
that Russia had by the leasing of Port Arthur
obtained the much desired ice-free port on the
Pacific, she must go further and secure railway
connexions between the port and the Siberian
Railway. The construction of the railway and
the towns along it was estimated to cost about
R. 100,000,000.

As the result of Count Muravieff's policy
the labours of Count Witte, who had sole
charge of the Russian finances, were doubled.
It was the urgent necessity of obtaining
money which sent Count Witte to the British
Minister with a proposal.

Count Witte's Proposal to Great Britain.

Count Witte said to the British representative: "Hitherto our policy has been to raise
national loans for political purposes in France
and Germany exclusively. The markets in
those countries are tightening, and we must
therefore seek a market for our national bonds
in your country. The British Government

appears, however, to have but very little influence over the money market, and so to make any issues a success we must first secure the goodwill of the British people. Russia is therefore planning to give your countrymen greater freedom to engage in the Russian coastal trade, to introduce British capital into industries, and other commercial privileges. We also propose to send a committee to London, to be permanently established there, and they too will try to secure the goodwill of the British public. We should like to have the British Government with us and give us all the help in its power to achieve our end."

Further developing his idea Count Witte proposed that a strong delegation of Moscow merchants should visit London for the purpose of studying the commercial situation and business conditions, and that later this visit should be balanced by a return visit from English merchants.

However, this proposal to exchange visits was dropped afterwards by reason of the attitude of the City of London, where public feeling ran high on account of indignation at the arbitrary methods adopted by the Russian Government to quell an insurrection in the interior of Russia.

Indeed, the whole proposition came to nothing at that time, for the British people were then very ill-disposed towards Russia. Even so, if the Russian statesmen had gone about their work in the right way they would have been able to reverse this feeling, for Russia was in a position to offer many favours to Great Britain.

APPENDIX

THE FUTURE POLICY OF JAPAN

(Summary of Articles in " Jiji Shimpo" in June and July, 1895.)

OUR countrymen must be warned that the Treaty of Shimonoseki and its amendments by no means end matters. We must be prepared for many years to come to carry on both warlike and peaceful measures for the assertion of our rights. We must not shrink from attacking both to the North and the South with that object in view.

As to the permanent occupation of Port Arthur, that port of Fengtien, which the second article of the Treaty of Shimonoseki gave to us, we have had to surrender it. The Russian, French, and German Governments considered our possession of it threatening to the peace of the Far East. They therefore advised our Government to hand it back to China, and as our only object has been the peace of the Far East, we decided to accept that advice and to return the Liaotung Territory. This is made quite clear by the Imperial Rescript.

It is naturally very unpleasant to relinquish something which has once been in our possession, and though we did this as the result of the friendly advice of the Powers, it seems an insupportable hardship that what we have once gained should be so lost.

Opinions may differ in connexion with this matter, but as I have always pointed out, the ways of international intercourse amongst the so-called civilized nations are inconceivably intricate.

If of course everybody is satisfied with the present state of affairs, then there is nothing more to be said. But as the proverb says, "To each ten men ten complexions," and it is only natural to expect that there will be many people who will be deeply dissatisfied with the turn which affairs have taken.

But there is no necessity to advise such people to smother their discontent, nor to persuade them to be contented, nor to seek to turn them to an amiable frame of mind.

It must never be forgotten that discontent is the prime factor which incites men to greater activity and diligence. We should therefore retain our discontent to spur us on to greater diligence, with a view to one day dispersing the gloom around us. We must persistently suffer the insufferable and support the insupportable for the sake of what the future will have in store for us. In this way we shall truly promote the strength and prosperity of our nation.

We should exert ourselves to develop our commerce and our industries, for these are the principal factors of national expansion. Commerce and industry produce wealth. We must also devote more attention than ever to building up on scientific principles our army and navy.

We must continue to study according to Western methods, for the application of science is the most important item of warlike preparations that civilized nations regard. If new ships of war are considered necessary, we must build them at any cost. If the organization of our army is found to be wrong, it must at once be renovated. If advisable our whole military system must be entirely changed. We must build docks to be able to repair our ships. We must establish a steel factory to supply guns and ammunition. Our railways must be extended so that we can mobilize our troops rapidly. Our oversea shipping must be developed so that we can provide transports to carry our armies abroad.

This is the programme that we have to keep always in view. We have suffered hard things, and we must suffer yet harder things before we arrive at our destiny. Whilst our preparations are in the making things will not be easy. Our taxes will increase, our people will suffer distress, our Government officials must work for small salaries, and amidst a discontented populace. Political parties will use the distress to raise political disputes, and our whole Empire may feel unhappy. But if we always keep in view the great ends which I have indicated, then we shall endure all these things gladly.

Peace has been restored, but it cannot be a lasting peace. We must sacrifice ourselves, we must work for those who come after us, we must face difficulties, even as "combing our hair in the rain and bathing in the wind." Many will be disappointed and discontented, but they must endure all their disappointment and discontent in silence and with a brave heart.

If they were private merchants they would endure and continue struggling. As a nation we must do the same. The actions of great Powers are like those of individual merchants. Each one seeks his own gain, and if he cannot at once win continues with increased energy until he does so at last.

The man who misunderstands the attitude of the Powers is a stupid clodhopper. It is no good being angry with a merchant because he sets his prices high. It is equally unreasonable to be angry with the Powers because their gain is our loss.

It is not the first time in history that a Power which has been strategically successful has been beaten in the Council Chamber. Russia beat Turkey, but England cancelled her victory and she returned home empty-handed, leaving behind the mountain of treasure for which she had fought.

On another occasion Russia was beaten in the field by England, but she was able to nullify all England's victories by her diplomacy.

No modern war except the Franco-Prussian War has been concluded without interference from some outside Power. Even America, which boasts of its isolation, keeps good watch on the events of the other States of both North and South America. No Power is to be blamed if it takes advantage of the weakness of another and can gain advantages for itself thereby.

The precedents of history teach us that no surprise should be evoked because Japan has been forced by a combination of Powers to evacuate the Liao-tung. Three Powers were banded against her, and it was in her own interests as well as to preserve peace that she followed their advice.

What Japan has now to do is to keep perfectly quiet, to lull the suspicions that have arisen against her, and to wait, meanwhile strengthening the foundations of her national power, watching and waiting for the opportunity which must one day surely come in the Orient. When that day arrives she will be able to follow her own course, not only able to put meddling Powers in their places, but even, as necessity arises, meddling with the affairs of other Powers. Then truly she will be able to reap advantages for herself.

If, however, the continental Powers are going to continue the Alliance against her in order to curb our just aspirations, to fulfil which we have poured out life and money, then we too must endeavour to ourselves make an alliance which shall counteract their machinations.

The recent change of Ministry in England seems likely to lead to a still further anti-Russian feeling in that country.

During the war with China, feelings in Japan were by no means friendly to England. Her arbitrary limitation of the area of hostilities was strongly felt by our military men, and it was on account of this that our plans for an attack on Nanking had to be based on Shantung.

England's attitude is, however, not difficult to understand, and when it came to the time of making peace her attitude veered from being strictly neutral to being rather friendly to us. True, she advised us to give way before the Three-Power Note, but this was not because she approved of the attitude of Germany, France, and Russia, but because she foresaw that if we were to resist war would result. But on the question of Formosa she strongly resented the

French attitude, and let us know that she preferred us to be in occupation of that island and not France. For this we must be very grateful to her.

Affairs in the Far East are now only in a preliminary stage. Russia certainly intends to obtain a predominating position, and in that case England's position in China might well become precarious. In this country all are agreed that the question must finally be settled by the sword, but England is not in a good strategical position for such a course, for the struggle would be settled on land and not on sea.

If, however, England and Japan should make an alliance the problems of the Far East would be already settled. If the events of the late war have proved to the English statesmen that China is merely a big idol, then they may in time come to realize that Japan, though she is young and inexperienced, is earnest and energetic. China is no longer the Power of the Far East, nor is Japan yet it. Russia is trying to be it. But the real Power in the Far East is England. If she casts her lot in with Russia she can no longer be it, for Russia can coerce China by land, which England cannot oppose. But if England casts in her lot with Japan, then she will more than ever be the Power of the Far East, for she is the deciding factor at present. England and Japan together can control China and ensure the maintenance of peace in the Orient.

CHAPTER III

The Friends of the Anglo-Japanese Alliance

I SHALL now go back to the point where I left off discussing the Anglo-Japanese Alliance, when I was at Count Ito's house. I had then said in reply to a question by Count Inouye that an Anglo-Japanese Alliance would be most desirable. I had pointed out that an alliance was in reality an exchange of benefits. But as Russia was a much richer country than Japan she would be able to offer much better terms to Great Britain, and consequently it would be a matter of considerable difficulty to bring about such an alliance as that under discussion. I had the facts about Russia which I have now related and I used them as the basis of my conclusions. I could only guess at the real attitude of Counts Ito and Inouye, but I formed the impression that they were in favour of an alliance with Great Britain.

In 1899 I was appointed Minister at London, and in 1900 took up my post there.

If I remember rightly it was in March, 1900, in the early part of the month, that I discussed the proposal for an alliance between Great Britain and Japan with Dr. Morrison, the famous correspondent of *The Times* at Peking, whom I met in the rooms above the *Jiji Shimpo* office at Tokio.[1]

Mr. (now Sir) Valentine Chirol, the Foreign Editor of *The Times*, visited the Far East twice whilst I was Minister at Peking, and I met him several times there and exchanged views with him. When I was returning from Peking I travelled on the same steamer with him. Ever since I have been in close contact with him, and he has always heartily favoured the idea of an Anglo-Japanese Alliance.

I knew a great number of newspaper men when I was in London, and the large majority have been in favour of an alliance.

In the year 1900 the Boxer trouble broke out in China, and the Legations in Peking were invested. Troops were mobilized from the different nations for the rescue of the Legations.

[1] The Count here refers to the Kojunsha Club, which forms part of the buildings of the *Jiji Shimpo*, and which was also founded by the late Mr. Fukuzawa. There is a private entrance to the club from the editorial offices of the *Jiji Shimpo*.—ED.

Pro-Japanese Sentiment in England.

At that time England was tired of war, that in South Africa having only just been concluded.[1] She could not very well stretch out her arms to the Far East. The people of England were very alarmed at the reports of the situation in China. When, however, they found that Japan had mobilized an army for the rescue of the Legations they were very much obliged to Japan and felt very relieved. I was received in audience by Queen Victoria at Buckingham Palace at this time for the purpose of presenting my credentials, and Her Majesty specially requested me to convey her thanks to the Emperor of Japan for the prompt dispatch of Japanese troops to China.

According to my judgment at that time, the pro-Japanese sentiment in England extended from the highest to the lowest and humblest citizen.

On the other hand, Russia was planning to occupy the Manchurian Provinces as a set-off to and as an indemnity for the Boxer outrages. Then began the infamous campaign of bloodshed along the Amur River.

England could not but feel rather resentful

[1] The South African War had not been concluded.—ED.

towards Russia. She realized the necessity of joint action with Japan in the Far East, and that proved to be one of the most important reasons why the Anglo-Japanese Alliance was later concluded.

However, no immediate steps were taken by either England or Japan. Although public sentiment in both countries greatly appreciated the idea of an alliance, the Governments of the two countries did not then enter into any serious negotiations for such an understanding.

CHAPTER IV

The Negotiations for the Conclusion of the Anglo-Japanese Alliance

IT was in March or April of last year (1901) that Baron von Eckardstein, who was then the German Chargé d'Affaires in London, called on me on several occasions. In the course of my conversations with him he expressed to me the opinion that nothing would prove more effective for the maintenance of peace in the Far East than the conclusion of a triple alliance between Japan, Great Britain, and Germany. He told me also that so far as he could learn many influential members of the British Cabinet, the Marquis of Lansdowne, Mr. Arthur Balfour, Mr. Joseph Chamberlain, and the Duke of Devonshire had been of this opinion for some time, and that lately the Marquis of Salisbury had also accepted the suggestion. So far as Germany was concerned, continued the Baron, the popular feeling against England was certainly very strong, but the German Government itself did not share this feeling. The Baron specially mentioned that two of the most distinguished dignitaries of the Empire were favourable to the idea of making an alliance between the three Powers. I presume that the two persons to whom he referred were the Kaiser and Count (now Prince) von Bülow. On the occasion of the funeral of the late Queen Victoria the Kaiser met King Edward several times at Osborne, and then Baron von Eckardstein always attended the Kaiser and so he was in a position to know the real circumstances. The Baron suggested that if the Japanese Government should take the initiative in formally proposing to conclude such an alliance the scheme would most certainly be crowned with success.

Even to-day I am still doubtful of the true object Baron von Eckardstein had in view in making the above proposals to me. Did he speak to me, suggesting such an alliance, because he had been so instructed by his own Government, or had he some other reason?

There was no doubt in my mind that if the British Government had an intention of entering into such an alliance as the German

Chargé had outlined, it would prove to be a combination of the utmost advantage to Japan. I also thought that it would be an advantage, and it certainly could do no harm, to find out the intentions of the British Government in the matter. I therefore applied to my own Government for its permission to try to do so. I was authorized by a telegram, dated April 16th of last year (1901), to sound the British Government, but to do so only on my own responsibility, and in such a manner as in no way to bind my Government, which expressed itself as not being in a position to give an opinion either for or against the idea.

The following day, April 17th, I had occasion to call on Lord Lansdowne, and in the course of the conversation I referred to the situation in China, and explained that the future of that country was a source of anxiety to myself and that I believed that it was a matter of urgent necessity for Great Britain and Japan to make a permanent agreement for the maintenance of peace in the Far East. I expressed this as being my own personal view. I asked the opinion of Lord Lansdowne on the point, and he agreed that it was advisable to elaborate some means for the purpose I had suggested. Owing, however, to the absence from London of the Premier, Lord Salisbury, the British Government could not at the moment consider this very important matter. Lord Lansdowne said, however, that he was quite willing to listen to me if I had any good suggestion to make as to its solution. As I was about to leave him Lord Lansdowne added that an agreement such as I had suggested would not of necessity be confined to two countries, but any other country might be admitted to it.

Considering this last statement of Lord Lansdowne in conjunction with those already made to me by the German Chargé d'Affaires, I came to the opinion that the British Government had already had occasion to consider the matter, and might even have gone so far as to seek the views of the German Government on the same. However, owing to the absence of Lord Salisbury from London, it was impossible to do anything further in the matter at that time.

I decided nevertheless to watch the attitude of the British Government and to renew my conversation with Lord Lansdowne when Lord Salisbury returned. I accordingly telegraphed in these terms to my Government. But I also thought that it would be difficult for my Government to form a sufficiently concrete idea of the conditions so as to be enabled to send me any precise instructions, as so far I had only been able to refer to the matter in a vague way. I thought therefore that it would be as well to have some sort of a basis on which to negotiate, and this would tend to hasten any negotiations that might result. Accordingly I suggested in my telegram that if my Government should decide to try to make an Anglo-Japanese Alliance, the following basic principles should be adopted, on which to negotiate:

(1) That the principle of the open door and the territorial integrity of China should be maintained.

(2) That no country should be permitted to obtain from China any territorial rights, beyond those already granted by China in published treaties.

(3) That Japan, having greater interests in Korea than any other country, should be allowed freedom of action in Korea.

(4) That should either party to the alliance become involved in hostilities with any other country, the other signatory should maintain neutrality in the struggle, but in the event of a third nation joining in the struggle and attacking a party to the alliance then the co-signatory should take up arms to assist her ally.

(5) That the existing Anglo-German Agreement with regard to China remain in force.

(6) That the terms of the alliance relate exclusively to Eastern Asia, and the sphere of its operations shall not extend beyond the limits of Eastern Asia.

The reply which I received from Tokio expressed no opinion on the terms which I had suggested, but paid particular attention to the possibility of an understanding having already been arrived at between Great Britain and Germany on the matter. This my Government considered very possible, in view of Lord Lansdowne's statement that such an agreement as I had suggested should not necessarily be confined to the two countries. I was therefore instructed that it was very necessary to find out whether any understanding already existed between England and Germany, and I was again ordered to do this on my own responsibility.

It was not until May 10th that Lord Salisbury returned to London, and letting a few days elapse I again called on Lord Lansdowne on May 15th. I asked him for his views on the agreement between Great Britain and Japan with regard to Far Eastern affairs, which I had suggested at our last meeting.

Lord Lansdowne said that, first, he would

like to have some idea as to my opinion as to the lines which such an agreement should follow. I replied that the policy of Japan towards China had been repeatedly declared and was to-day the same as it was in the declarations, namely, the maintenance of the open door and the territorial integrity of China. As regards Korea, we only wished to maintain our interests in that country. I added that in my opinion the interests of Great Britain and Japan in China · were identical, and I reiterated that I thought it of the utmost importance for the two countries to stand together against any combination of other countries. Lord Lansdowne replied that the discussion of the main lines of an agreement was easy, but the difficulty would arise when details came to be settled. He said, however, that he would refer the matter to Lord Salisbury, and tell him my views, and he again repeated that the proposed agreement would not necessarily be confined to Great Britain and Japan, but a third country could also be admitted.

Next day Baron von Eckardstein called to see me, and told me that he had visited Lord Lansdowne just after I had seen him (Lord Lansdowne) on the previous day. The British Foreign Secretary had told him the purport of the conversation which he had had with me.

I telegraphed to Tokio, reporting the details of my conversation with Lord Lansdowne, and at the same time recommended that the Japanese Cabinet give the matter very careful consideration. Meanwhile a Cabinet change had taken place in Tokio. The fourth Ito Ministry collapsed and Prince Ito had resigned the Premiership on May 10th, being replaced by Marquis Saionji as temporary Premier. His appointment was, however, quickly followed by another change, and on June 2d Viscount (later Prince) Katsura was appointed Premier. M. (now Baron) Kato was replaced as Foreign Minister by Viscount Sone, who also held the office of Minister of Finance.

On account of these changes at Tokio and the confusion which ensued I received no answer to my telegram, and as I received no communication from Lord Lansdowne I was obliged to let the matter rest.

On July 15th, Sir Claude MacDonald, the British Minister at Tokio, who was then in London on leave of absence, unexpectedly called to see me, and told me that in an audience which he had had with King Edward VII. a few days previously His Majesty had expressed the opinion that it was necessary

GENERAL MARQUIS KATSURA, PRIME MINISTER OF JAPAN

for England and Japan to come to an understanding in some way or another, and it was
desirable that it should not be a merely
temporary understanding. Sir Claude even
went further and said that he had seen Lord
Salisbury, whose views on the matter went
beyond those of the King. His opinion was
that an alliance must be made between Great
Britain and Japan which would provide that
in the event of two or more countries com-
bining against one of the parties to the
alliance then the ally should assist the party
attacked by force of arms. Sir Claude said
that the British Government had the idea of
making such an alliance, but as this would be
a departure from the long-established policy
of the country in foreign affairs the negotiations of such an agreement would take some
time, and Lord Salisbury was a little afraid
that in the delay Japan and Russia might
form an alliance. Sir Claude added that
Baron von Eckardstein had been to the
Foreign Office and expressed fears that Japan
might make an alliance with Russia.

After I had considered my conversation
with Sir Claude I came to the conclusion that
his object in calling on me and in referring
so specifically to the question of the proposed
Anglo-Japanese Alliance was to pave the

way for the opening of serious negotiations, and that his visit had been inspired by instructions from Lord Salisbury. I therefore telegraphed to my Government the details of my conversation with Sir Claude, and added that as the British Government was nervous of a possible alliance between Japan and Russia, if my Government would hint that Japan and Russia would combine if there were no prospects of the successful conclusion of the proposed Anglo-Japanese Alliance, the British Government would be stimulated into making a favourable agreement.

What Sir Claude MacDonald actually said in his conversation with me was: "Whilst we are wasting time in discussing the terms of an agreement with Japan, the Japanese Government might take up the idea of making an alliance with Russia. In fact, the German Ambassador (? Chargé) has been to the Foreign Office and said that there was a possibility of such action on the side of Japan."

To this I replied: "As you know, the feelings of Japan are not friendly to Russia, but are friendly to England. Of course sentiment should be subordinated to considerations of actual profit, and without doubt if Russia should see her way to make substantial concessions to Japan, then certainly our feelings of enmity to that country would disappear."

It appeared to me that Sir Claude Mac-Donald was expressing opinions formed by Lord Lansdowne after a consideration of my views, and was striving for the materialization of what I had said about an Anglo-Japanese Alliance. Considering his remarks, I came to the conclusion that the British statesmen sincerely desired an alliance treaty, but were fearful of the conclusion of a convention between Japan and Russia. I thought, therefore, that we might take advantage of that fear on England's part, and by pretending that an agreement would be negotiated with Russia hasten on the conclusion of the treaty with Great Britain. Consequently when I telegraphed to Tokio the details of my conversation with Sir Claude MacDonald I also telegraphed my own views as I have expressed them above.

I saw Lord Lansdowne on July 31st, when the following conversation took place. He said: "We think that the time has come to discuss seriously the question of making a permanent treaty with Japan. I want, therefore, to ask you what is the view of the Japanese Government with regard to the relationship of international interests in Man-

9

churia, and secondly what sort of treaty you would want to make with us."

My reply was: "In my opinion the interests of Japan in Manchuria are only indirect. But, if Russia should one day occupy a part of Manchuria and extend her influence in those parts, then she would be able to absorb Korea, against which Japan would be obliged to protest. What Japan wants is to prevent Russia from coming into Manchuria, and if to do this she should be involved in war with Russia she wants to prevent a third party coming to the help of Russia. As for our general policy in regard to China, we wish to maintain the principle of the open door and to maintain the territorial integrity of China, as I said at our last conversation."

Lord Lansdowne answered: "As regards Korea, England has very little interest in that country, but she does not wish to see Korea fall into the hands of Russia. As regards China, our policy is identical with Japan's, namely, the maintenance of territorial integrity and the open door. I believe that in time we might adopt measures for the mutual protection of our interests in Eastern Asia. Now, please tell me, when Russia proposed to make Korea a buffer state, why did Japan refuse to agree?"

I replied: "With regard to Korea, it is quite useless to attempt to hold a neutral position. The Koreans are totally incapable of governing themselves, and we can never tell when civil war may not break out. In the event of civil war, who will hold the reins of government? It is after all very natural that the international interests in Korea should be conflicting."

At this point Lord Lansdowne interjected the remark that the situation between Japan and Korea was very similar to that which had obtained between Great Britain and the Transvaal. Lord Lansdowne said that my views were a suitable basis for discussion, and he would refer them to Lord Salisbury with a view to negotiations for a definite agreement being commenced.

I telegraphed this conversation to the Foreign Office in Tokio, and on August 8th received the following telegram in reply:

"Japanese Government acknowledges the purport of the propositions made by England regarding a definite agreement and accepts *in toto* your reports of your conversations with Lord Lansdowne. It desires you to proceed to obtain full particulars of the British attitude in this matter. Success or failure of this convention depends on your carefulness. When our policy is fully decided upon the work will be easy."

Of course I felt delighted when I received this telegram. Indeed, I had never felt happier in my life. I had a further interview with Lord Lansdowne and went into further details with him. As I had not yet received the power of plenipotentiary to conduct the negotiations with him, I continued to speak with him as a private person.

On August 16th Lord Lansdowne went to Ireland for a holiday. Before he left London, however, he told me that he would give the matter his most careful consideration during his holiday, and he asked me meanwhile to get the power of plenipotentiary from my Government. Matters therefore remained in abeyance for a time whilst I telegraphed to Tokio for the power of plenipotentiary.

In Tokio a change had taken place at the Foreign Office. On September 21st Count Komura had been appointed Foreign Minister. On October 8th he sent me the following telegram:

"The Japanese Government has carefully considered the question of the proposed alliance with Great Britain, and has formed a definite policy supporting the same and approving the course taken by you as pre-

COUNT KOMURA, JAPANESE MINISTER FOR FOREIGN AFFAIRS

viously telegraphed. Hereby you are given power to exchange officially views with the British Government in regard to the same."

Having thus received the formal power of plenipotentiary I was ready to commence the real negotiations.

On October 16th, Lord Lansdowne having returned to London, I called on him at the Foreign Office. Our conversation on that day resulted in the drafting of the preamble of the treaty.

Our conversation was briefly as follows: "Although," I said, "I have received the formal power of plenipotentiary to negotiate the treaty, I have not yet received the instructions of my Government about details. Under these circumstances would you object to my continuing to discuss the matter for the present as a private person, which would save a loss of time?"

To this Lord Lansdowne replied: "As I understand from your remarks that though you have the formal power of plenipotentiary from your Government to negotiate the treaty, you are as yet not in possession of full instructions from your Government with regard to details, I am therefore quite willing to have our conversation regarded as personal, and that what you may say shall not be taken as binding on your Government."

I thanked him and said that we could discuss the matter, and my home Government could afterwards instruct me as to any alterations which they might desire.

The Marquis again agreed and then said: "As the first thing in making an agreement is to ascertain the views and wishes of the other contracting parties, I would like to know officially what are the wishes of Japan in this matter."

I said in reply to Lord Lansdowne: "My country considers as its first and last wish the protection of its interests in Korea, and the prevention of interference by any other country in Korea."

"What, then, next," asked the Marquis, "is your policy in China?"

I answered: "As I have before stated, we entirely agree with the British policy in that country. That is to say, we wish to maintain the territorial integrity of China and the principle of equal opportunity."

"Very well," said Lord Lansdowne; "now, what sort of a treaty do you think that Great Britain and Japan should enter into?"

I said: "The nature of the alliance should, in my opinion, be, that in the event of one of the allies appealing to arms to realize the above objects, the co-signatory to the treaty should maintain and observe neutrality, but if another Power or other Powers should aid the enemy country, then the allied Power should at once take up arms in aid of its ally."[1]

To this Lord Lansdowne replied: "What you ask appears to me to be reasonable. We think, however, that the treaty should be on broader lines than you suggest, and that aside from the specific conditions which you have mentioned and which would be embodied in the treaty, Great Britain and Japan should always maintain the closest friendship and connexion, especially in respect to Far Eastern affairs, and in regard to those we should exchange views without reserve and act throughout in a concerted manner. We think that that is very important."

I agreed with this proposal, but I thought that Lord Lansdowne wanted to tie us down beforehand so as to prevent us from entering

[1] There is a striking difference between the above MS. version of Count Hayashi's proposed terms of the alliance and the version published in the *Jiji Shimpo*. The latter version said: "We should like a treaty so that if another country should attack one of the allies, and a third country should go to the assistance of the hostile country, then the non-belligerent ally shall go to the help of the attacked ally."—ED.

into any engagement with another country, once we had signed the proposed treaty of alliance with Great Britain. I said that the wishes of my country would be the same, and the Marquis ended the interview by saying that he would report all I had said to Lord Salisbury, and that as soon as they had carefully studied the matter he would discuss it with me again.

Before leaving the Marquis I asked him: "What are your plans with regard to including Germany in the agreement?"

He replied: "We think that it will be best to negotiate with you first and then later we can invite Germany to join in the negotiations and come into the alliance."

The reason why I asked about Germany was because I was uncertain as to the relationship of England and Germany on the matter, and I wanted, as my Government had instructed me, to find out whether or not there was a definite arrangement between England and Germany that the latter country would have to be invited to join in the treaty.

I had various other conversations with Lord Lansdowne following on the one above, and I was quite satisfied that the British Government regarded the proposed alliance seriously.

On November 6th Lord Lansdowne handed me the first draft of the proposed treaty. It was as follows:

"Desirous of maintaining the present state of the affairs in the Far East, of preserving the general peace, and in especial of preventing the absorption of Korea by another country, and of maintaining the independence and territorial integrity of China and of securing to every country equal commercial and industrial privileges in China, the Governments of the two allied nations have agreed upon the following articles:

"(1) If either of the two nations (Great Britain and Japan) shall be engaged in war with another foreign country for the object of protecting the interests mentioned in the foregoing, the allied nation shall maintain a strict neutrality and shall endeavour to prevent any other nation from supporting the hostile country.

"(2) If, in the conditions mentioned above, another foreign country shall join the enemy of the allied nation, then the two allied countries shall make common war, and peace shall only be concluded with the mutual consent of the two allies.

"(3) The allied nations shall not enter into any agreement with another country affecting the interests of the allies in Korea without mutual consent.

"(4) In the event of Great Britain or Japan at any time considering the interests mentioned above as being jeopardized, then the Governments of the two countries shall communicate together fully and frankly without concealment."

Lord Lansdowne asked that the Japanese Government should most carefully study this draft and said that he thought that it fully covered all I had said about Japanese interests in Korea.

He then said: "In the Cabinet Council, when this draft was discussed, two or three members expressed the opinion that Japanese interests in Korea are very great, in fact much greater than British interests in the Yangtse. They felt, therefore, that the treaty as it is outlined there would be rather one-sided and too much in favour of Japan. They suggest, therefore, that its scope be extended so as to bring our Indian interests under it. I would like you to consider this point and later let me know your opinion about it."

The above draft showed no material difference from the substance of my conversations with Lord Lansdowne. There was, however, one very important point about it. It said that no foreign country should absorb Korea. But it did *not* say that Great Britain recognized Japan's paramount interests in Korea, and it gave no assurance that Great Britain would not interfere with Japan in any action she might feel called on to take to protect her interests in Korea.

I felt that this was the whole essence of the treaty and must be made clear, and if Great Britain was likely to feel embarrassed by putting a clear statement in the treaty, then it must be covered by a secret treaty. I, therefore, telegraphed to Tokio, sending with Lord Lansdowne's draft my views on the same.

On November 13th I received the following instructions from Tokio:

"Regarding the draft treaty the Government will communicate its decision as soon as reasonably possible. In the meanwhile go to Paris and meet Marquis Ito and communicate to him all the telegrams exchanged with regard to this matter, and try to get his support to the British draft. Telegraph the result of your conversation with him immediately."

I must now say something in explanation of Marquis Ito's appearance in Europe.

Some weeks previous to this I had received a private communication from home stating that a Genro (Elder Statesmen) Council had been held at the residence of Count Katsura, the Premier, presumably in connexion with the suggested Russo-Japanese Agreement, and it had been proposed that on the occasion of Marquis Ito's visit to America he should be entrusted to proceed to St. Petersburg to conduct the negotiations to conclude the proposed agreement.

I had learned from newspaper statements that the intended visit of Marquis Ito to America was for the recovery of his health, and to receive the honorary degree of LL.D. on the occasion of the hundredth anniversary of the foundation of Yale University.

On receiving the above-mentioned private communication I felt that as the Acting Minister of Foreign Affairs, Viscount Sone, had sent me telegraphic instructions on August 8th to initiate negotiations for the conclusion of an Anglo-Japanese Alliance, there should have been no reason for the Premier to contemplate a Russo-Japanese Agreement, or even to agree to the contemplation of such an agreement by others.

Of course the Russo-Japanese Agreement might not be irreconcilable with the Anglo-

Japanese Alliance, but as the latter was already in course of negotiation it would be most inopportune to negotiate simultaneously with Russia, inasmuch as such an agreement as a Russo-Japanese one ought only to be concluded after mutual consideration and after the conclusion of the alliance.

I thought, therefore, that the private communication which I have mentioned really only dealt with a rumour. At all events if Marquis Ito should proceed to St. Petersburg I might have an opportunity of meeting him in Europe first, and as there was no necessity to keep the matter secret from him, I could speak to him fully and frankly of the affairs in connexion with the negotiations with England.

I did not, therefore, pay much attention to the private communication to which I have referred, but went on with the negotiations for the alliance, and steady progress was made in the *pourparlers*. Though I had informed the British Government that it was my private individual opinions which I was presenting, all the proceedings were reported to my home Government, and the Foreign Minister had assured me that all my actions would be duly approved. Still, I felt that as long as the instructions sent me on August 8th and October 8th were in force, whereby

I was empowered to exchange views with the British Government, the proposal that Marquis Ito should visit Russia ought to be suspended, if he had not already left Japan, or if he had already started he ought to be recalled from America. If the Government wished to conceal the Anglo-Japanese negotiations from Russia, some other means should have been found not involving such dangers and risks.

Marquis Ito had just arrived in Paris when I received the telegram of November 13th, quoted above. He had proceeded directly from America to France without coming to England, presumably as the result of orders to hurry on the negotiations for the Russo-Japanese Agreement.

I had thought that the Marquis should preferably pass by England, as otherwise it might attract public attention. On the following day, therefore, November 14th, I proceeded to Paris and submitted all the telegrams to the Marquis and reported to him the details of the negotiations I had been carrying on with Lord Lansdowne in regard to the proposed alliance.

In the various manuscripts of the *Memoirs* there are two different versions of the conversations with Marquis Ito in Paris. As they differ in important details it is considered best to give them both.—Ed.

Version as given by " Jiji Shimpo."

The following is a summary of the conversations which I had with Marquis Ito in Paris. He told me that before he left Japan he had seen Marquis Yamagata, Count Inouye, and other Genro, and also the Premier, Count Katsura, and the Acting Foreign Minister, Viscount Sone. In his opinion it was unprofitable for Japan and Russia to continue to look at each other with "cross eyes" in regard to Korea. It was urgent that a compromise should be effected, and it was therefore decided that Marquis Ito should go from Yale to Russia, taking with him M. Tsusuki as his diplomatic assistant, and at St. Petersburg discuss the Korean problem. At the time of his departure from Japan the Government had not considered the negotiations with England as being serious. It did not really believe that an Anglo-Japanese Alliance was possible.

The terms on which the Marquis was to negotiate in St. Petersburg were as follows: Russia was to have a free hand in Manchuria and Japan to have a free hand in Korea. Both Powers were to agree not to establish a naval base at Masampo.

This was as much as it was dared to ask for.

Whilst I was in Paris Mr. Tsusuki told me

that M. Kurino had accepted the post of Minister at St. Petersburg on condition that power was given him to conclude a convention with Russia.

Marquis Ito was much puzzled at my mission to him in Paris. He had had no idea that the negotiations with Britain had progressed so far and he was at a loss to know what to do.

I was in the same dilemma. Here was I negotiating with Lord Lansdowne, getting out plenipotentiary powers from Tokio to negotiate an alliance, and yet the Government at home had sent Ito to negotiate a convention with Russia. If M. Tsusuki's statement with regard to Mr. Kurino was true, the matter was even more outrageous. I thought that it was most inconsistent of my Government to have telegraphed accepting my views with regard to an Anglo-Japanese Alliance and then to take such steps.

I therefore telegraphed from Paris to ask the Government to reflect on the affair. The answer which I received was as follows:

"The Government has not changed its policy and Kurino has been given no such mission."

When I received this telegram and showed it to Marquis Ito he was still more puzzled.

The Marquis realized, however, that the negotiations with Great Britain had reached such a point that the Japanese Government could not withdraw. So after further discussion it was arranged that he should support the Anglo-Japanese Alliance in principle, and I only gained this point after employing much persuasive oratory. It was further agreed that he should continue his visit to Russia, as his coming had already been announced to the Russian Government.

I agreed not to give any reply to the British Government with regard to the draft treaty until after I had heard from the Marquis, after his arrival in St. Petersburg.

MS. Version.

The Marquis, discussing my report of the negotiations with Lord Lansdowne, said: "It had been my intention to proceed to America for a visit, and before starting I met Marquis Yamagata and Count Inouye at the residence of the Prime Minister, Count Katsura. There were also present at the meeting other persons, including Viscount Sone, the Acting Foreign Minister. The three statesmen, Yamagata, Inouye, and Katsura, said that a consultation must be made with Russia

10

as further complications with that country would not be endurable. They requested me to take the opportunity of my visit to America to proceed as far as Russia, and there to take such measures as might suit the occasion. I felt it a nuisance to have to go to Europe, but I accepted their request, anyhow, without considering much what would be the outcome. I am now informed by you of the Anglo-Japanese Alliance negotiations, which have made such progress that withdrawal from them is no longer possible. It is contrary to my anticipations."

That evening, November 14th, the Marquis dispatched a telegram to the Japanese Government, stating that he adhered to the principles of the proposed Anglo-Japanese Alliance.

The next day the Marquis told me that as the *pourparlers* for the Anglo-Japanese Alliance had made such progress he thought that he would rather return to Japan without proceeding to Russia, but, on the other hand, as preliminary notice had been given to Russia of his intended visit, he must go to St. Petersburg. He said, however, that he would endeavour to do nothing there which might disturb the Anglo-Japanese negotiations.

M. Tsusuki, who accompanied the Marquis as his diplomatic assistant, seemed to favour a Franco-Russian-Japanese Alliance or Agreement. Moreover, he informed me that report had it that M. Kurino was to be appointed Minister at St. Petersburg, and that as he (Kurino) had asserted for a long time that he would accept the St. Petersburg post only on the condition that he were permitted to negotiate a triangular treaty, it must be presumed that he had received instructions to conclude such a treaty.

I was very greatly surprised at this news. As I have stated, it might be difficult to predict which would be the more preferable, a Franco-Russian-Japanese Treaty or an Anglo-Japanese Treaty, but I for my part was confident that the latter would be preferable.

As according to my instructions I had good reason to believe that my Government was of the same opinion as myself, I had been able to make good progress with the negotiations in London. Since the telegraphic instructions had been sent to me on October 8th the British Government, in spite of my non-committal declaration of October 16th, seemed to have recognized that I had certainly been acting under instructions from my home Government.

Whilst the Anglo-Japanese negotiations had on the one hand reached to such a point, one of the Elder Statesmen had been dispatched to St. Petersburg with the object of concluding an agreement with Russia. Even if it were pretended that his visit was only an ordinary trip in his private capacity, no one in England would believe it.

Then there was also to be considered the statement about M. Kurino, that he was empowered to make a triangular arrangement between Japan, Russia, and France. If that was true the success of the one policy must inevitably lead to a loss of confidence in the other.

After carefully thinking the matter over I dispatched a telegram to the Foreign Minister on November 18th on the subject, and on November 19th received the reply. This absolutely denied M. Tsusuki's statement, and said that the Government had no intention whatsoever of withdrawing in any degree from the position it had taken up in regard to the proposed treaty of alliance with Great Britain, and that the instructions given to M. Kurino had merely been to endeavour to obtain a settlement of Korean affairs, and that similar instructions would be given to any Minister who might be accredited to Russia.

[End of MS. version.]

Later I received a communication on the subject from M. Kurino, but in it he did not appear to recognize the true significance of the telegram sent me from Tokio.

I returned to London on November 19th.

In spite of the reassuring telegrams which had been received by Marquis Ito and myself from Tokio, I was still much perturbed over the business, especially as Marquis Ito was still going on to St. Petersburg. After my arrival in London, therefore, I telegraphed to the Marquis in the following terms:

"So long as it is our policy to conclude a Russo-Japanese Convention we should adopt one or other of the following courses: first, conclude the Anglo-Japanese Treaty, then notify Britain of our intention to negotiate a convention with Russia and proceed to the conclusion of the convention; or, secondly, so long as the Anglo-Japanese negotiations in London are in progress, you shall not discuss a convention with the Russian statesmen, unless they first propose it. In that case you must put them off as best you can."

I felt that it would be most risky to attempt to introduce Machiavellian tactics into either the Anglo-Japanese or Russo-Japanese negotiations. When Marquis Ito received my telegram he replied assuring me that he would adopt the second of the two courses formulated by me.

The day after my return from Paris I saw Lord Lansdowne, who asked me for the reply of the Japanese Government to the draft of November 6th. I had to tell him that I had not yet received the reply and he then said that there was grave danger in delay, as the news of the proposed treaty might leak out and obstacles might then be raised.

I said that I would telegraph to Tokio, asking them to hasten their reply.

The Marquis then asked me about Marquis Ito's visit to Russia and expressed a wish that he should come to England. He appeared to be rather annoyed that he had not done so. He said that if it was the intention of the Japanese Government to negotiate a convention or agreement with Russia whilst the negotiations with Great Britain were in progress the British Government would be very angry.

I replied that an alliance was quite a new departure in Japanese policy, and therefore it was necessary to study the proposal very carefully. That was the reason for the delay which had occurred, and as for the visit of Marquis Ito to Russia, that had no special meaning at all. I said that the Marquis could not come to London in November, because in that month the London climate was at its worst, and fogs were general, and would prejudice Marquis Ito's health, which was not good.

Lord Lansdowne evidently did not think very much of my explanation. He knew quite well that Marquis Ito had travelled across the Atlantic from America to France. He (Ito) had given out that he was travelling for his health. Why, if he was travelling for his health, did he go to St. Petersburg in the winter? The British Foreign Minister was very dissatisfied with my explanation of the Marquis's movements.

After I had left Lord Lansdowne I met Mr. Bertie, the Under-Secretary of State, who was much more outspoken and came immediately to the point. He asked me straight out if Marquis Ito had any intention of trying to negotiate an agreement with Russia, and when I denied this he said:

"If the news of our negotiations with you were to leak out and come to Russian ears, Russia would most certainly try to make an agreement with you, and perhaps offer you what at first sight would appear to be more advantageous terms. But," he added, "you could not rely on those terms, for Russia would certainly repudiate them whenever it appeared to suit her." I said that I thought that this was very probable. "Well," said Mr. Bertie, "I want to warn you to be very careful." I promised that I would be.

It was, of course, very natural for Lord Lansdowne, Mr. Bertie, and others to talk in this manner, and it was just because I knew the state of mind of these men that I had telegraphed to Marquis Ito the day before to be sure not to make any negotiations with Russia, when he should arrive at St. Petersburg. I was strongly convinced, from the mere fact of my being approached with conversations of the above tenor immediately on my return from Paris, that the British Government was closely watching the movements of Marquis Ito in Europe.

After my return from the Foreign Office I telegraphed to Tokio, stating what were the conditions in England and reporting my conversations with Lord Lansdowne and Mr. Bertie, and I strongly advised the Japanese Government to proceed with the negotiations with Great Britain, and to drop all idea of a convention with Russia until after the conclusion of the treaty of alliance. I also sent a copy of this telegram to Marquis Ito, in order that he might be warned to be very careful to confine his conversations with the

Russian statesmen to ordinary topics, and leave Russia as soon as possible.

Marquis Ito telegraphed to me in reply that he fully recognized the necessity of proceeding with the Anglo-Japanese negotiations, and that he would be most careful not to touch upon any vital issues in the conversations which he might have with the Russian authorities.

I also received a telegram from my Government saying that the Japanese Government had no intention of playing a double game as between Britain and Russia, and definitely stating that Marquis Ito had no official mission in St. Petersburg, which information I was instructed to give to Lord Lansdowne, if the matter came up again in the conversations between us. The telegram concluded with the statement that the Foreign Minister was sick and unable to deal with affairs of State for the moment, but the Government's reply to the draft agreement would be sent as soon as possible.

Both these pieces of information I conveyed to Lord Lansdowne, and he expressed his satisfaction that Marquis Ito's visit to Russia was not an official one.

On November 30th the Tokio Government sent me by telegraph the following amendments to the draft of the treaty which Lord Lansdowne had handed me on November 6th.

In the preamble it was proposed that the words "Far East," should be changed into "Extreme East," and the words "China" and "Korea" into "Chinese Empire" and "Korean Empire" respectively, whilst the words "or any part thereof being occupied" were to be inserted after the words "absorption of Korea."

In the second article, "another country" was to be changed into "one or more foreign countries."

In the third article, "affecting the interests" should be changed into "jeopardizing the interest."

The following was to be added as a fifth article: "The alliance shall continue for five years from the day of signature, and if the high contracting parties so desire it may be further continued thereafter. In case the term of the alliance shall expire during a war, then the alliance shall be continued in force until peace shall have been restored."

The following was to be added as a special provision: "Great Britain shall recognize Japan's right to take the necessary steps for the protection of her interests in Korea."

Together with the foregoing amendments my telegraphic instructions from Tokio read:

"The Government has presented the proposed amendments before the Throne; His Majesty the Emperor referred them to the Elder Statesmen remaining at this time in Tokio for their opinion on them; His Majesty also asked for the opinion of Marquis Ito now in Europe. You shall attend to this matter over there. But in order to keep the amendments absolutely secret, you shall send a member of the Legation staff to St. Petersburg, and he shall take to Marquis Ito a copy of the amendments in cipher, and this shall be deciphered only after his arrival in St. Petersburg. He shall give the amendments to Marquis Ito for his advice on them."

Almost immediately after I had received this telegram came another informing me that Count Komura had given the following note to the British Minister at Tokio, Sir Claude MacDonald:

"The Japanese Cabinet, after making slight amendments in the original draft of the treaty as proposed by the British Government, has decided to accept that draft. The nature of the amendments is such as we believe that the British Government will not object to accept. The Cabinet, before dispatching the amendments to London, had presented them before the Throne."

Obedient to my instructions I sent M. Matsui,[1] Secretary of the Legation at London, to Russia to Marquis Ito. M. Matsui arrived in St. Petersburg on December 3d, and having deciphered them showed all the telegrams to Marquis Ito. The latter did not at that time make any particular comment on the amendments, but it was stated to me afterwards that he was very pleased indeed with the telegram in which it was stated that his Majesty had asked for his advice.

Marquis Ito thought that it was rather hasty of Count Komura to have communicated with Sir Claude MacDonald with regard to the amendments, and he was rather displeased about this. He told M. Matsui that he would study the amendments very carefully, and let him know his opinion on them when he should arrive in Berlin from St. Petersburg.

He then asked M. Matsui whether he knew that there was a telegram from Count Inouye.

M. Matsui replied that he had not heard of such a telegram in London. Marquis Ito then showed M. Matsui a telegram from Count Inouye to the Marquis in which he advised the latter to make a careful study of the rela-

[1] Vice-Minister of Foreign Affairs, 1913.—ED.

tions between Germany and Russia before he should send home any opinion about the Government's proposed amendments.

Before the Marquis left the Russian capital he applied for an interview with Count Lamsdorff, and this he received on December 4th. That same night he left Russia for Berlin. M. Matsui, so as not to attract attention, left St. Petersburg one day later and rejoined the Marquis in Berlin. He remained in Berlin with the Marquis for three days and returned to London on December 11th.

In Berlin M. Matsui heard for the first time of the objections which Marquis Ito had not only to the amendments but also to the alliance itself. They were as follows:

"In both the British draft and also in the Japanese amendments to it," said the Marquis, "there are words to the effect that the absorption of Korea by a foreign country shall be prevented. But in Korea only Japan and Russia have interests of any importance. England has no interests there. In regard to Korea the proper thing to do is to make a convention with Russia, and settle the problem of that country. Even if we make an alliance with England it is not certain that we shall reap much benefit from it.

"Besides this, according to the draft, England will attain the same position in Korea as Japan has already. It really means giving to England a position in that country which she has not now got. From this point of view I consider that the proposal is unreasonable.

"Again, even if we have another country joining in the alliance, as Germany, we shall only be giving to that country the same as we are giving to England. That country also will obtain a new position in Korea which she had not got before. Consequently the proposed instrument would be doubly bad.

"The Japanese Government certainly ought to make some proper amendments with regard to all that touches Korea. The Government at Tokio may have been led to propose such hasty amendments by promptings of the British Government, but nevertheless such a serious matter ought not to be concluded without very careful consideration. We ought also to study carefully the whole question of the international relations between the European nations. Count Inouye's telegram shows that whilst all the members of the Cabinet have agreed, he himself has not hastily thrown himself on the side of the proposed alliance. According to his opinion, first, it is difficult to understand why England has broken her record in foreign politics and has decided to enter into an alliance with us; secondly, the mere fact that England has adopted this attitude shows that she is in dire need, and she therefore wants to use us in order to make us bear some of her burdens; thirdly, Germany in Count Inouye's view may not enter the alliance. It is for these reasons that the Count has telegraphed to me asking me to reconsider the relations between the European Powers and only then to form my opinions.

"Now, my views coincide with Count Inouye's, and I have therefore telegraphed home to the Count that such a serious matter as the Anglo-Japanese Alliance should not be decided hastily, and also I have telegraphed my opinions on the proposed amendments, just as I have expressed them to you, M. Matsui.

"Now," continued the Marquis, "what we ought to pay special attention to in connexion with this problem is, in my opinion, the attitude of Russia. I think that all negotiations for an Anglo-Japanese Alliance ought to be suspended until we are quite sure that it is hopeless to attempt to conclude a convention with Russia.

"I am convinced from what I have seen

and heard in the Russian capital that the
attitude of that country is at least rather
conciliatory towards Japan, and it appears
to me that she is sincerely desirous of co-
operating with us to settle the Korean question.
Count Witte, the very day after I arrived in
St. Petersburg, came to call on me, and proposed to me to discuss Far Eastern affairs
with an open heart. Count Lamsdorff was
also very polite to me, but especially I was
struck by the words used by the Emperor
in the audience which he graciously granted
to me. At the very beginning he spoke of
the urgent necessity of Russia and Japan
working harmoniously together, and he said
that it was his wish that some sort of an
agreement should be arrived at between the
two countries.

"I met Count Witte again after the first
interview, of which I told you. He then
spoke in the characteristic diplomatic manner
repeating the stereotyped declaration that
Russia and Japan should work harmoniously
together.

"I, however, cut him short and told him
that vague generalities would not help matters,
for the crux of the situation between the two
countries lay in Korea. I said that if both
countries were going on struggling for supre-

macy in Korea the inevitable result must be friction. I said to him: 'If your country really wishes to work harmoniously with Japan you must give us a free hand in Korea, commercially, industrially, and politically. And more than that, if civil war breaks out in Korea we must have the right to send our troops over there to restore order. Without that there can be no question of Russia and Japan working in harmony.'

"Count Witte agreed with my views altogether. He said to me that Russia would recognize our privilege of sending troops to Korea, and would give us freedom of action in that country. But he said that if Russia did that then Japan must undertake not to maintain large forces in Korea, which would amount to an occupation of the country.

"When I met Count Lamsdorff I spoke about the same subject. He was not so well disposed to my views as Count Witte had shown himself. He said that what I wanted virtually amounted to a protectorate over Korea, from which Japan would gain everything and Russia nothing. He agreed, however, to consult his colleagues on the matter and promised to send his reply to me at Berlin.

"In addition to these conversations," Marquis Ito continued to M. Matsui, "I have

11

made an arrangement to communicate privately both with Count Lamsdorff and Count Witte, and to write to them on the matter from time to time. As the result, therefore, of my informal conversations in St. Petersburg we are in a position to commence formal negotiations with the Russian Government through the Japanese Minister at St. Petersburg, and this we can now do at any time. That is the situation in regard to Russia at this moment, and in my opinion the prospects of our being able to make a satisfactory convention with Russia are very favourable.

"I think that the time is premature for making a co-operative agreement with England. I have, therefore, telegraphed in this sense to both Count Inouye and to Count Katsura, giving them full details of my conversations with the Emperor and the Russian statesmen. Why, in the Council of Elder Statesmen before the Throne on December 7th, it has been unanimously decided in favour of an Anglo-Japanese Alliance I do not know. But perhaps my telegram had not arrived in time. Anyhow, please convey my views to Baron Hayashi and tell him that I want him to let me know what he thinks before he presents the Japanese amendments to the British Government."

The foregoing is a summary of what Marquis Ito said to M. Matsui and what M. Matsui reported to me.

In the telegram of August 8th sent me by the then Acting Foreign Minister, Viscount Sone, it was stated that the Government had decided favourably with regard to the British proposal for a treaty. I had since been informed that this sentence had been inserted at the express request of Marquis Ito. And when I saw the latter in Paris he had in principle approved the Anglo-Japanese Treaty, and had promised to confine his conversation in St. Petersburg to generalities. He had again repeated this promise in his telegram to me after my return from Paris, and again in his reply to my telegram reporting Lord Lansdowne's suspicions with regard to his visit to Russia. Yet, in spite of all these promises, as soon as ever he met the Russian statesmen he had plunged into conversations on the most delicate of matters. It was indeed most inconsistent of him. Just where his mind really dwelt it is impossible to say. I could not comprehend his views on the Japanese Government's amendments to the draft treaty, which he had telegraphed to Tokio and which were sent to me.

I came to the conclusion that they contained nothing which should affect the desirability of the alliance, and that the Government, also taking that view, had passed them by.

The truth with regard to the Marquis was that he just changed his mind, which was not uncommon for him. In Tokio he was amongst persons of conflicting views, some for and some against the alliance. When he saw me in Paris I had persuaded him to my view. When he got to St. Petersburg the statesmen told him in diplomatic language how easily the Korean question could be settled if he had charge of the negotiations, and so he changed his mind again. Perhaps he is not so much to be blamed.

I was even more puzzled about Count Inouye's telegram to the Marquis to study German-Russian affairs. As far as I could see it had nothing to do with the matter, nothing on earth. It raised from the very beginning the whole question of the general advisability of the alliance, and the time for considering the broad general desirability of the alliance was long past. So worried was I at Marquis Ito's attitude that I telegraphed a statement of the whole matter to Count Komura, the Foreign Minister.

Before, however, my telegram was received

or even dispatched the Government had already obtained the consent of the Elder Statesmen, assembled in Council (*i. e.*, Council before the Throne on December 7th[1]), and on December 10th Count Komura had tele-

[1] At the time of the publication of the summary of these *Memoirs*, by Reuter's Agency, the following note was attached: In connection with the Council before the Throne on December 7th, Reuter's Tokio correspondent recently heard from an authentic source an account of that Council.

His informant said: "Ito in Europe and Inouye in Tokio had been working hard for a Russo-Japanese agreement. Ito was dispatching furious telegrams daily to the Government and to Inouye on the matter. Finally a Council before the Throne was to be held to decide the question.

"The Cabinet were all in favour of supporting Hayashi in London, and indeed so strong was the sentiment that both Katsura and Komura informed their colleagues that in the event of the Emperor deciding against them and in favour of Ito they would resign office.

"At the Council, reports were submitted to his Majesty with regard to the Anglo-Japanese negotiations and then with regard to Ito's Russian negotiations. After reading them and studying them His Majesty turned to a Secretary and said: 'Go to the Imperial Cabinet and get Marquis Ito's report on a proposed Anglo-Japanese Alliance when he was Prime Minister.' When the report was brought the Emperor looked through it, and then turning to the Council said: 'In this report Marquis Ito, when Prime Minister, most strongly advised that an Alliance be made with Great Britain, and nothing has happened to change the situation during the last few months.' The Mikado then ordered Komura to instruct Hayashi to go ahead with the negotiations and then to telegraph to Ito to stop all negotiations with Russia.

"The Cabinet were really against Ito's proposals from the very beginning, but were willing to use him as a lever on England in order to hasten the negotiations; besides this, Ito and Inouye were far too powerful to be estopped from their attitude by anything less than an Imperial command."—ED.

graphed to me instructing me to present the amendments to Lord Lansdowne. At the same time I received a further telegraphic explanation of the amendments.

Marquis Ito having asked me to communicate with him before presenting the amendments, I communicated with him, and at the same time telegraphed as stated above to Count Komura, also asking the Government's views on Marquis Ito's representations.

The answer which I got from Count Komura was as follows:

"The instructions which you have received to present the amendments to the British Government were sent to you after a consultation of the Cabinet with the Elder Statesmen, and after careful consideration of Marquis Ito's views, and with the sanction of the Emperor. You will therefore fulfil your instructions immediately."

The meaning of this telegram was very clear to me. It signified that the Cabinet and the Elder Statesmen had totally rejected Marquis Ito's opinions and that the Anglo-Japanese Alliance was to be carried through, and I was of course very pleased.

I therefore went to the Foreign Office on the next day, December 12th, and presented the amendments to Lord Lansdowne, and also explained to him the reasons of each amendment. On December 16th I met the British Foreign Minister again, and on January 30, 1902, the treaty was signed.

In this manner the opposition of Marquis Ito to the Anglo-Japanese Alliance came to nothing, although even after his return to Japan he had hopes of the conclusion of a Russo-Japanese Treaty or Convention, as he had suggested in his conversations in St. Petersburg.

On December 12th, after he had received my telegram, saying that I was ordered to present the amendments, he realized that his opinions had been rejected by the Emperor, for he telegraphed to Prince Katsura as follows:

"My proposals appear to have been rejected. I can now only hope that room will be left for the speedy conclusion of a Russo-Japanese Convention with regard to Korea. I hope that you will keep the treaty of alliance with Great Britain in strict secrecy. Should that instrument be published it would create a very bad impression amongst the continental nations."

Now I shall tell a little about the negotiations between Lord Lansdowne and myself, after I had handed him the amendments to the draft treaty.

It would only be confusing to follow the proceedings chronologically, and it might be difficult to make quite clear the views of the two Governments if I proceeded by dates. I shall, therefore, take the completed text of the Treaty and shall tell you about the articles, taking each in turn.[1]

In the text of the draft treaty of November 6th is the following: "Desirous of maintaining the present state of affairs in the Far East, of preserving the general peace, and in especial of preventing the absorption of Korea by a foreign country, and of maintaining the independence and territorial integrity of China and of securing to every country equal commercial and industrial opportunities in China, etc."

Now the cardinal principle of the alliance had been declared by both Japan and Great Britain to be that outlined in the above, and there had been no question raised on that principle during the negotiations. But in the wording of the above there was a very slight difference of opinion. In the original draft of the British Government there was the phrase about wishing to preserve Korea from being absorbed by a foreign Power. But this referred only to the possible occupation

[1] Appendix B.

of the whole country, and so the Japanese Government, wishing to cover the eventuality that a portion of the country might be occupied on some pretext or other, asked that words to that effect should be inserted, as I related in telling of the first amendments sent from Tokio.

Then in the British drafts stood the words "China" and "Korea," which we asked to be changed into Chinese Empire and Korean Empire respectively, so as to cover the whole territories of each Empire.

The British Government made no objection to these alterations, but as the original wording, "to prevent the absorption of Korea by a foreign Power" and "to maintain the independence and the territorial integrity of China," made some discrimination between the two countries, the British Government in January, 1902, presented us with a new draft, containing amendments with regard to these points, and we accepted their amendments.

Article I. of the treaty said: "Japan has special interests in Korea, politically, commercially, and industrially," as proposed by the British Government. But we wanted Great Britain to give us a free hand in Korea, and therefore when we presented the first amendments in December we inserted, as a separate provision: "Great Britain recognizes Japan's privileges in Korea," as I have told you. We considered this recognition to be most important. Indeed, it was for us the most important thing in the Treaty. The discussion of this amendment took up most of the time of the negotiations.

On December 16th I saw Lord Lansdowne with regard to the amendments, and the following conversation took place.

Lord Lansdowne said: "This is a very difficult matter, because if we put in your special provision which you want to cover Japan's interests in Korea, it would mean that Japan would be virtually given a free hand in that country. You know that would mean friction with Russia and possibly end in a war between all the Powers."

I replied that it was unthinkable that Japan would lightly engage in an armed conflict with Russia. If we were to lose it, then we should find it no easy task to recover from the losses which such a struggle would inflict. We wanted the British Government to trust to the common sense of the Japanese. Besides, according to the new draft a party to the alliance is not called on to help the other party unless a second or third party should attack the ally. Even if Japan and Russia should engage in war we thought that it would be a little far-fetched to believe that it would lead to a general conflagration.

To this Lord Lansdowne said: "Well, suppose now that we put it that Japan pledges herself to consult Great Britain with regard to any action she may take in Korea?"

I said at once that this would be quite impossible. "Russia," I said, "acts spasmodically and it is quite impossible to foresee or know beforehand what she is going to do next. We, too, should have to act promptly, in order to be able to meet any emergency which might arise. If we had to consult you each time there was necessity of action, delays would ensue and the opportunity to do something effective might be lost. For example, a few years ago Russia tried to lease a strip of land at Masampo. We, however, beat Russia in the matter and leased that strip of land ourselves so that Russia could not have it. The same thing might happen again, and time would be the essence of success."

Lord Lansdowne said that he was afraid there would be criticism of the sphere of influence of the alliance, for England would gain much less under it than Japan would.

He said that the interests of England along the Yangtse were far less important than those of Japan and Korea.

I replied to this: "I do not agree to that. In the amount of trade done and also in the area of territory affected the interests of Great Britain are far greater. Besides, those districts are to-day at peace, but danger lies dormant there, and it should by no means be underestimated. If the present viceroys should be removed or die there might easily occur along the Yangtse a greater rebellion than that of the Boxers. In that case the alliance with Japan would be of inestimable value to Great Britain."

Lord Lansdowne said that he would consult about it and let me know at our next meeting.

When I left Lord Lansdowne I telegraphed this conversation to Tokio, for I felt very doubtful of what the British Cabinet might think about the proposal. I suggested that our Government should send the British Government some definite assurance that we did not want a free hand in Korea as a basis for future aggression.

On December 19th, just before the meeting of the Cabinet at which the matter was to be discussed, I received the following assurance with instructions to hand it immediately to Lord Lansdowne:

"Even if Japan should have free action in Korea, the British Government may rest assured that the Japanese Government has no intention of using that freedom as a means of aggression. Until now Japan's policy in Korea has not only not been aggressive, but has been peaceful. The Japanese Government wishes to point out, however, that disturbances in Korea are liable to occur with great suddenness, and in consequence it would be necessary for Japan, in defence of her interests, to act equally promptly. Whilst the Japanese Government has every desire to consult with Great Britain it would not be altogether possible to do so, owing to the resultant loss of time, whilst communications were being exchanged. Japan realizes her responsibilities towards Korea, and her policy towards that country will be in strict conformity with the Nishi-Rosen Convention."

Using this assurance as a basis, I at once wrote a memorandum to Lord Lansdowne on the subject, and sent it over to him. He actually received it whilst at the Cabinet meeting.

When I saw him afterwards, however, he said that there was still objection to the special provision which we had proposed. He said that the wording of it was not sufficiently clear, and some members of the Cabinet considered that the wording might be construed as meaning that Great Britain was assisting Japan in aggression on Korea. He suggested that it might be better to insert some suitable words in the preamble and drop the special provision altogether.

I telegraphed home about this, but our Government thought that it might be difficult to get the matter covered in the preamble and telegraphed to me:

"Instead of putting the provision in the preamble, which may be awkward, suggest to the British Government that there be an exchange of diplomatic notes, wherein it shall be declared that neither Japan nor Great Britain have any ambitions or designs on Korea, but that Great Britain recognizes the privilege of Japan to take the necessary steps in order to protect and promote her interests in Korea."

I communicated this proposal to Lord Lansdowne, but he did not care for it, and he made a counter-proposal by means of an altogether new draft, which was communicated to me on January 14th, and which I at once telegraphed to Tokio.

Text of the Second British Draft.

"Great Britain and Japan, desiring the present status maintained in the Extreme East, and considering that it is imperative to preserve the independence and territorial integrity of the Chinese Empire and of the Korean Empire, and to permit every nation to have equal opportunity in commerce and industry in China and Korea, hereby agree together as follows:

"Article I.   Great Britain and Japan both recognize the independence of the Chinese Empire and of the Korean Empire, and declare that they have not any aggressive tendencies in those countries, provided, however, that since the Japanese Government has called the attention of the British Government to Japan's special commercial as well as political interests in Korea, and the British Government has drawn the attention of the Japanese Government to Great Britain's special interests in China, in the case of those interests being jeopardized by other nations or whenever there is danger of invasion by a foreign country, then the two nations shall have the privilege of taking the necessary steps for the protection of those interests.

"Article II.   If Great Britain or Japan

shall engage in war for the protection of the interests mentioned in the foregoing article, the other ally shall keep a strict neutrality and shall try to prevent any other nation from joining the enemy.

"Article III. In case the foregoing situation arises and another nation should join the enemy, then the other ally shall immediately help its ally in war, and peace shall be concluded only by mutual agreement.

"Article IV. The allies mutually agree not to conclude any agreement with any other nation, which might prejudice the mutual interests of the allies, without consultation between them.

"Article V. Whenever Great Britain or Japan shall deem that the above-mentioned interests are jeopardized, then they shall freely and frankly without reserve communicate with each other.

"Article VI. This treaty shall be effective immediately after its signature, and shall continue in force for a period of five years.

"If neither of the allies should inform the other twelve months before the expiration of the treaty of its desire to cancel the same on its expiration, then the treaty shall remain in force for twelve months from the day of expiration, provided, however, that if the expiration should occur during a war then the treaty shall remain in force until after peace be restored.

"Duly empowered by our respective Governments, we hereby attach our signature and seal to this declaration."[1]

When Lord Lansdowne handed me the second draft he said: "This draft has been prepared in order to prevent any attack in Parliament on the Cabinet on the ground that the preservation of the territorial integrity of China and the prevention of the absorption of Korea are two things which cannot be considered as of equal importance. In addition to this, the actual purport of the notes you have handed me at various times embodying the views of the Japanese Government, has been embodied in these articles. I hope, therefore, that your Government will agree to thi draft. With regard to the signature and publication of the treaty we propose to make a public announcement after consultation with the Japanese Government. I may add that various members of

[1] It has to be remembered that the drafts given in this volume probably differ from the official drafts at the Foreign Office in wording, owing to their being translated from the Japanese. As, however, Count Hayashi declares that they are based on the official records, there can be no reasonable doubt of their substantial accuracy as regards tenor.—ED.

the Cabinet raised objections to the special provision in Article I., and I hope you will give me credit for having got it put in."

When I received this draft I thought that it embodied all the concessions which the British Government was likely to make, and as it contained all the points raised by my Government, I expected that the Japanese Government would agree to it. I, therefore, immediately telegraphed it to Tokio and asked for the Government's approval.

To my surprise, however, my Government sent me the following protest:

"Everything in the new draft is satisfactory except Article I. According to the wording in that article, 'Japanese Government . . . in Korea' and 'British Government . . . in China,' it appears as though Japan is to abandon her interests in China. Delete, therefore, the sentence after 'the Japanese Government' and substitute the following: 'Taking into consideration the fact that Japan has special political and commercial interests in Korea, and also the fact that Great Britain and Japan have special interests in China, the British and Japanese Governments allow each other to take the necessary steps to protect the interests of each, in case there is any danger of those interests being jeopardized.' In explaining the reason of the amendment to the British Government you will say that Japan has at least as many interests in China as Great Britain has, and you should remember that the Japanese Government cannot agree to any clause or article setting aside Japanese interests in China."

I showed this amendment to Lord Lansdowne and explained to him what my Government had telegraphed about Japanese interests in China.

The Marquis said: "That is of course true, but we want to make it as unnoticeable as possible, as otherwise the treaty may meet with opposition in Parliament. We shall have to consult further about the point."

The Marquis then continued: "According to the Japanese amendment the phrase 'whenever there is danger of invasion by a foreign country' is deleted. This phrase was inserted by Lord Salisbury with the special object of preventing Great Britain from being dragged into the maelstrom in case of Japan, on account of an aggressive policy in Korea, being involved in war with a foreign country. It was approved by the Cabinet, and if we try to alter it now, it might prove very difficult to secure the approval of the Cabinet."

I refuted this argument by saying that there was sufficient safeguard against it in the first words of Article I., by which both nations denied having any aggressive intentions.

Still the Marquis would not agree. He said: "If the words at the beginning of Article I. really and truly express the desires of the Japanese Government, then I think that the Japanese Government ought not to raise any difficulties with regard to the insertion of the words desired by the British Cabinet. I will be very pleased if you will inform the Japanese Government of our view and obtain their opinion about it before the next meeting of the British Cabinet."

I telegraphed to Tokio exactly what the British Foreign Minister had said and received the following reply:

"The reason why the phrase regarding the danger of invasion by a foreign country has been struck out is because we are apprehensive of the interests of Great Britain and Japan being trampled on in the event of internal disturbances in China and Korea. In that case we are bound to consider the situation created as being the same as if our interests were attacked by a foreign country. If, however, the British Government is willing to agree to the insertion of a phrase covering the possibility of internal disturbances, we shall be able to agree to the phrase about danger of invasion."

I at once conveyed the sense of this instruction to Lord Lansdowne. He said that there would still be a good deal of opposition in the Cabinet to a phrase covering internal disturbances, for such a phrase might be taken to signify interference with the internal affairs of an independent country, which was an attitude entirely foreign to British policy and interests.

I said, however, that China and Korea could hardly be considered as being in the same category with other countries, and history had shown that internal disturbances were a frequent and peculiar condition of those countries. I narrated to Marquis Lansdowne the numerous instances of revolution in Korea in the 15th and 16th years of Meiji (1882–3) and the instances of trouble in China from the time of Tung Shue Tong right down to the Boxer Rebellion.

I said to Lord Lansdowne: "These disturbances may occur at any moment, and if Great Britain and Japan are going to make an alliance we might as well arrange in it for all eventualities." I pointed out, too, that though the words in the draft, "invasion by a foreign country," appeared to be quite plain, yet in practice they would not prove to be so, and it might be very difficult to decide whether a certain action by a foreign country was or was not invasion. I said: "Consider the ancient histories, wherein there are many instances in which nations at war call the enemy invaders, yet the onlookers could not really tell, as we say, 'which crow was male, and which female,' and only historians, hundreds of years afterwards, have been able to decide which combatant was really the invader. I think that if we do not make some such provision as that suggested we may not be able to accomplish the fundamental object of the alliance."

Nevertheless the Marquis was still obdurate and replied that he would carefully consider the matter. He showed me his private draft of the amendment, and said that he would send me another draft after he had consulted with Lord Salisbury.

On January 24, 1902, he sent me another draft, which had been approved at the Cabinet meeting on that day. In the new draft the amended passage read as follows:

"Whenever there is danger that these interests are jeopardized by other nations or there is need of intervention in order to protect the lives and properties of the subjects of the allied countries, then the two nations agree that they shall allow each other to take the necessary steps." We had no objection to offer to this amendment, except with regard to one or two words. We had further conversations with regard to these, and very quickly we came to a complete agreement, and cleared up all the difficulties of Article I.

It was arranged that our interests in China should be covered by inserting this phrase: "On the part of Japan, in addition to her interests in China, her interests in Korea," etc., and so Article I. was agreed upon as it stood in the completed treaty.

The question of Japan's interests in Korea had thus been completely settled. As for the points embodied in Articles II. and III., namely, that in case one of the allies engages in war with a third nation the other shall maintain neutrality, and if another country helps the enemy then the ally shall take up arms in defence of the first-mentioned ally, these points had been discussed and agreed on in my first formal negotiations with Lord Lansdowne, and so there was very little negotiation with regard to them.

With regard to the article prohibiting the

negotiation of any special agreements during the continuance of the alliance there has been no serious difference of opinion. The sentence in Article IV. of the treaty and the sentence in Article V., namely, "The allies agree not to enter into any special agreement with any other nation, which might prejudice the interests mentioned in the foregoing articles without mutual consent," and, "If Great Britain and Japan should agree that the above-mentioned interests are in jeopardy, the two Governments shall communicate together fully and frankly," had been covered by my conversation with Lord Lansdowne at the opening of the formal negotiations when he had said that Japan and Great Britain should always maintain intimate friendship with each other, and in regard to the problems of the Extreme East shall exchange views without reserve and shall take joint action in defence of their interests. As a result of this early understanding no objection to this point was raised.

On the other hand, in the first British draft there was a phrase that in regard to China and Korea no agreement should be made with any other country. We, in our first amendments, changed it so as to read that no agreement should be made which might be prejudicial to the interests of the other party. The British Government offered no objection to this amendment.

I think that the object of our amending the draft in this manner was that in the event of our entering into some agreement with another country, with regard to our interests in China or Korea, we should not be compelled to inform Great Britain at the time of negotiation. If we had been obliged to do so it might have been very inconvenient for us. For example, whilst I was actually negotiating with Lord Lansdowne over the treaty of alliance, our Government, as already narrated, had sent Marquis Ito to St. Petersburg and had even appointed M. Kurino as our Minister to St. Petersburg with a view to negotiating a Russo-Franco-Japanese Agreement. That was the reason why we made the amendment.

Regarding the term of the alliance, as set forth in Article VI., there had been no provision for this in the British draft of November 6th. I had telegraphed to my Government recommending it to make the term for five years, to be renewable for a further period of five years on the expiration of the first term. The Government practically adopted my suggestion. Thus this matter was settled and inserted in Article V. of the first draft amendments.

Another point, that of continuing the alliance, in the event of its expiration during a period of war, was also satisfactorily settled at the same time. The British Government made no objections to either of our suggestions on these points, but in their second draft of the treaty they slightly changed the method of renewing the life of the treaty, by inserting a sentence that unless one of the allies should give a year's notice to terminate the treaty it should automatically remain in force indefinitely but subject to a year's notice from either party. The Japanese Government had no objection to that.

I have previously narrated that the British Foreign Minister, as the result of agitation by some members of the Cabinet, wished to extend the scope of the alliance so as to include the protection of British interests in India in case of necessity.

The arguments advanced by Lord Lansdowne for this were, briefly, that Japan under the treaty obtained protection for her enormous interests in Korea, but Great Britain only obtained protection for her interests in the Yangtse Valley. If these were compared Japan's interests were far greater, for they were vital to her. In order, therefore, to obtain more equilibrium in the advantages which the treaty gave, Japan should agree to include Great Britain's interests in India and their protection among the mutual objects of the alliance.

I believe that Mr. Chamberlain felt strongly on this point.

Anyhow, when our Government considered the matter it was not willing to include India in the scope of the treaty, and it was for this reason that in the first British draft it amended the words "Far East" into "Extreme East," and then there could be no doubt on the point. The argument which it sent to me for my instruction was as follows:

"The original object of the alliance is to protect the mutual interests of Great Britain and Japan in the Extreme East, that is, in China and Korea. Judging from the declarations of other Powers on the subject in reference to China, they also feel that they have interests in that country. So, by declaring our intention of maintaining the existing status in China, the alliance between Japan and Great Britain is a document of importance to all Powers, for not only does it protect the interests of Great Britain and Japan in China but also the interests of every other country having interests in China. The alliance is, therefore, impartial to all nations. But if we now extend its scope to cover India then it would be going beyond the original intention of the two signatories, and it could no longer be regarded by other nations in the same impartial manner. For this reason we cannot agree to the British proposal."

When I received this argument I thought that it looked very plausible, but on examination I came to the conclusion that it was very feeble. I thought this because whilst the argument with regard to international interests in China was correct, the introduction of the protection of Japanese interests in Korea was just as much outside the field of impartiality as the British proposal was supposed to be. I felt that if I were to attempt to argue the point with Lord Lansdowne on the lines laid down by my Government it would be just like "poking a bush to produce a snake."

When I discussed the point with the Marquis, therefore, I argued differently. I said: "If we extend the sphere of influence of the alliance we may be obliged to meddle with various complicated interests, and thus we may be obliged to step outside the objects originally intended when the alliance was proposed. Our Government would much prefer to limit the application of the alliance to our interests in China and Korea."

Later in the negotiations Lord Lansdowne again referred to the Indian proposition. He said: "I am afraid there will be criticism that the benefits derived by Japan and Great Britain are not proportionate."

To this I could only repeat what I had said before, namely, that British interests along the Yangtse were in no way behind those of Japan in Korea, and that should disturbances arise in those districts, then the benefit which Britain would derive from the alliance would indeed be very great. I told Lord Lansdowne that in the event of the development of necessity, the Japanese Government would certainly act in regard to India in the manner in which the British Government would desire, and the matter was left like that.

A very important matter which had to be settled was the question of whether Germany should be invited to enter the alliance. This question had been in suspense since the beginning of the negotiations, and to tell the truth it had been rather worrying both the British and the Japanese Governments. Marquis Ito had been strongly of the opinion that we should not keep the negotiations secret until after the conclusion of the treaty, for he said that if we thus excluded Germany and merely gave her the chance to join in the alliance after the conclusion of the negotiations, we should get only very hard feelings from that country.

On November 20th, the day after I had returned from my visit to Paris to consult with Marquis Ito, I asked Lord Lansdowne for his opinion on the matter. He said then: "Germany certainly recognizes that the interests of Great Britain and Japan in China are very large and that her own interests do not bear comparison with those of the two nations; even if we do not inform her until the negotiations are concluded it does not necessarily follow that she will be vexed. Besides, if we inform Germany about the alliance too soon she may use it as an instrument to advance her own interests. I think that it would be better to wait before we inform her of it."

Later, however, the Marquis raised the question himself to me and asked: "What shall we do about letting Germany come into the alliance?"

I replied that I believed our Government had the intention of proposing to Germany after consulting the British Government on the matter, but only when the treaty had been concluded.

I telegraphed to Count Komura on the point and he replied:

"The Imperial Japanese Government desires that Germany should eventually enter the treaty. But, until either the treaty has been finally signed or until all the articles have been finally agreed on, we think that it is better to keep the whole matter secret. It would, therefore, be advisable to postpone notifying Germany until later. We consider, however, that as Great Britain, in comparison with Japan, has far more important relations with the Powers and particularly with Germany, the matter of notifying Germany should be left to the discretion of the British Government."

I agreed with this view, and I was also afraid that if Germany should be notified she might utilize her participation in the treaty to obtain some special interest for herself under it. I, therefore, communicated my views and those of my Government to Lord Lansdowne. He at once agreed to my Government's attitude, and was indeed very satisfied with it. Soon after that the negotiations were brought to an end and I received instructions from Tokio to sign the treaty and seal it.

Then our Government seemed to recognize that there might be some necessity for inviting Germany to participate in the treaty and telegraphed to me:

"We have left the question of inviting Germany to the discretion of the British Government. However, we would like to have Germany come into the treaty, but if an invitation is to be extended to her it should be done by the British and Japanese Governments simultaneously. Inquire from the British Government when notice is to be given to the British Ambassador at Berlin to notify the German Government."

I communicated this message to Lord Lansdowne.

It happened just at that time that the German Imperial Chancellor, Count von Bülow, had made a speech in the Reichstag, attacking Mr. Joseph Chamberlain, the British Colonial Minister, and he had also used some derogatory language with regard to the British army. As a result, the British people, who had been getting very irritated with the German Press on account of its attitude in the South African War, now became seriously hostile to Germany. Lord Lansdowne thought that the moment was hardly propitious for approaching Germany, so it was decided to wait a little. Later, however, he thought it might be better to informally notify Count von Metternich, the German Ambassador in London, not giving him the text of the treaty but only an outline of the same. He consulted me about this, and explained that this step would prevent Germany from raising objections later on. He also thought that by this it would be possible to gauge the views of the German Government on the matter.

I telegraphed to Tokio asking my Government's opinion, and as a result it was decided to notify the German representatives at London and Tokio in the same manner on the same day, February 3d.

Well, on the night of February 2d Lord Lansdowne hurriedly sent me a messenger with a message that he had decided for certain reasons to postpone notifying the German Ambassador, and asking me to telegraph to Tokio to postpone the notification there.

I calculated the difference in time between London and Tokio and the time necessary for drafting, coding, transmission, and de-coding, and found that indeed I had no time to lose if the message was to get to Tokio in time.

13

So I sent the telegram as an urgent official dispatch, but all was in vain. The Foreign Minister, Count Komura, before he had received my telegram had already informally notified the German Minister of the treaty. So the British Government had in its turn to notify informally the German Ambassador. Afterwards I heard that the postponement of the notification was desired on account of some wish expressed by King Edward.

Anyhow nothing happened, for our notification to Germany was only a notification, and was not an invitation to join the treaty. It does not appear either that Germany really wanted to be a party to it. It may have been due to the strained relations between Great Britain and Germany at that time. Or it may be that the German Chargé d'Affaires who had been at one time so enthusiastic about the matter had felt only a temporary enthusiasm and the matter had been forgotten altogether. Or again it may have been that owing to the relationship between Russia and Germany the latter had decided that there was no advantage in joining in the alliance.

In 1899, after the Anglo-German Convention about China had been concluded, and even whilst the ink was wet, Germany declared that Manchuria was to be regarded as outside the sphere of that Convention. That showed plainly the real feelings which Germany had at heart. On account of the strained relations between Great Britain and Germany we certainly took no special steps to induce her to join in the alliance, but, on the other hand, if Germany had been really sincere in her earlier overtures and had proposed to come into the alliance, a triple alliance might easily have been concluded. It is not reasonable to suppose that Germany was purposely excluded by Great Britain and Japan.

As I have said, the first article, that referring to Japan's interests in Korea, took up most of the time of the negotiations.

That article was agreed upon on January 28, 1902, and on the same day the remainder of the articles were also approved. On January 29th I received a telegram from my Government giving me authority to sign and seal the instrument.

On January 30th, at 5 P.M., at the British Foreign Office, the Marquis of Lansdowne and I signed the treaty.

There was a little difference with regard to the formalities observed. The British Government was of opinion that all those officials participating in the signature should be empowered to sign by power of attorney from their respective Governments. Our Government, however, was of the opinion that as there were no ratifications to be exchanged it was not necessary to obtain power of attorney, and the British Government accepted this view.

After the signature of the treaty, the Tokio Foreign Office published the text of the treaty on February 12, 1902. This date had to be selected on account of the public holidays, otherwise it would have been published earlier. The British Government published the treaty on February 11th. As a rule a treaty of alliance is kept secret. The British Government had not intended to publish the text of the treaty officially, but to let it leak out in an indirect method. Our Government maintained that since the treaty was not aimed at any one nation as an enemy, and that as its objects coincided with the policy declared by all the Powers in regard to China, namely, the maintenance of the principle of equal opportunity and the territorial integrity of China, no harm could be done by the publication of the entire document. On the other hand, if it were kept secret, it might tend to create wild rumours as to the sphere of influence of the treaty, and this might be injurious to the mutual interests of the allies.

We, therefore, thought that it was better to publish the document, and the British Government agreed to our opinion.

Of course, once the treaty was signed and sealed it would have been much more difficult to keep it secret. Especially if Germany was to be notified it would be difficult. On the other hand, its publication could have a very salutary effect on the Manchurian situation, which was then a very prominent question in the Extreme East.

Our Government, when it had been decided to publish, proposed to do so on February 12th. That day in England was a Wednesday, which was then private business day in the British House of Commons, and Government business could not be handled in consequence. The British Government proposed, therefore, to publish the treaty on February 11th, and we would have done the same, but it was Kigensetsu, an important Japanese holiday, which made it impossible. It was, therefore, published on different days in England and Japan as described.

Our Government, of course, sent to the Governments of the various Powers copies of the treaty, through our Ministers abroad.

The different Governments were all satisfied with the treaty, and replied to our notes that they considered the peace of the Extreme East would be more securely safeguarded by the conclusion of the treaty.

Only the Russian Foreign Minister was astonished to see such words in the treaty as "war" and "engaged in war." He thought that very extraordinary. He had never dreamed that there ever could be such a thing as a war in the Extreme East, and so he was much astonished to find that such an eventuality was provided for.

By the way, there was a connexion between the contents of the treaty and its announcement. If the treaty were to be kept secret there was not so much need to make trouble about the wording of Article I. But if it were to be made public, then such expressions had to be chosen as would not invite the criticism of outsiders. That is why the negotiations over this clause took such a long time.

I have now written the history of the negotiations for the Anglo-Japanese Alliance. It was a great pleasure for me to sign this treaty, and it was a great success for Japan. But I do not think that our Government behaved well over it, especially in regard to sending Marquis Ito to St. Petersburg whilst I was negotiating with Lord Lansdowne. He ought not to have been sent whilst the negotiations with Great Britain were in progress. Besides the embarrassment which it caused me in my negotiations, as the conversations with Lord Lansdowne and Mr. Bertie showed, such a lack of faith and breach of honour put Japan in a very bad predicament. She has indeed won the support of Great Britain, but she lost the respect of Russia and of other European countries.[1]

[1] With regard to the publication of the treaty, Count Hayashi makes no reference to perhaps its most extraordinary incident. Three days before the treaty was officially published, the *Yorodzu Choho*, a very sensational Tokio evening paper, came out with the full text of the treaty. It created a considerable stir in Tokio, but it was denied by the authorities, whilst amongst others who were interviewed by the journalists, Baron v. Rosen, the Russian Minister, vehemently denied the possibility of such a treaty being entered into. The full story of how the treaty leaked out has never been published, but I have heard that the German Legation gave hint of it to a certain Akimoto, who was connected with the *Yorodzu*, and he obtained the full text from a clerk in the Foreign Office.—ED.

CHAPTER V

Later Notes on the Alliance

[The following additional notes on the Anglo-Japanese Treaty were written by Count Hayashi in 1907 or 1908.—Ed.]

As has been stated elsewhere, the visit of Marquis Ito to Russia was apparently an ordinary pleasure trip. Nevertheless, the various Governments must have at once conjectured the true object of the journey, and no doubt his arrival was impatiently awaited in Russia.

The proposal of the Marquis to proceed to Russia (after my interview with him in Paris on November 14th) but to do nothing to prejudice the negotiations for the Anglo-Japanese Treaty was a difficult one to carry out. I saw that it was necessary to sound the depth of the Marquis's resolution on the point, and, therefore, I wrote to him on November 21st to Berlin, where he was then

staying. He replied to me on the 24th, con-
firming his opinion of the necessity of an alliance with Great Britain, and enclosing a copy
of a telegram, endorsing the alliance, which
he asked me to send on to the Japanese Government, if I approved of it. This telegram
was at once dispatched to Tokio.

When the Marquis arrived in St. Petersburg
the Russian Government, as might have been
anticipated, at once proposed a Russo-Japanese Agreement. The Marquis was now placed
in a dilemma and seems to have experienced
a very real hardship in the matter.

In Japan a Genro Council was held in this
connexion early in December. At this Council
Marquis Inouye was reported to have opposed bitterly the proposal for an Anglo-
Japanese Alliance on the ground that its
conclusion would place Marquis Ito, who had
gone to Russia for very different purposes,
in a most difficult position. At the time I
received a report to the above effect from
indirect sources, but there is no doubt now
that such was the position taken up by Marquis Inouye. Anyhow, various opinions were
raised at this Council for and against the
alliance.

Marquis Ito, as I have related, left St.
Petersburg and arrived in London on De-

cember 24th. He left London for Paris on January 7, 1902, and started on his homeward journey (*via* Suez).

Meanwhile M. Kurino, the new Minister to St. Petersburg, had arrived in Paris, where he had already been accredited. As he had so many friends in France, such as M. Hanotaux, the ex-Minister for Foreign Affairs, and others, he seems to have exposed his own political views to certain persons in official circles. When Marquis Ito arrived in Paris, M. Kurino met him and Baron (then M.) Tsusuki, and was greatly surprised to hear from the latter about the negotiations for an alliance with Great Britain. This was the first he had heard about it. He seems to have been quite unaware of any such negotiations having been in train previous to his departure from Japan. Yet the draft of the proposed treaty of alliance must have reached the Foreign Minister prior to his departure for Paris, and the Foreign Minister, perhaps as the result of certain circumstances which then existed, had evidently told him nothing about the matter.

The Anglo-Japanese Treaty was signed on January 30th, and it was published in London and Tokio on February 11th and 12th. The enthusiasm shown in both countries at the publication was good evidence that the alliance accorded with public opinion both in England and Japan.

According to what we learned indirectly, the Russian Government believed that Marquis Ito had been sent to St. Petersburg to sound the intentions of the Russian Government in regard to a Russo-Japanese Agreement, and that having ascertained the views of the Russian Foreign Office, he had to go to Paris to confer with M. Kurino, who, on his arrival in St. Petersburg, would be authorized to commence the formal negotiations. Consequently the Russian Government was very much disappointed at the publication of the Anglo-Japanese Alliance, which occurred just prior to M. Kurino's arrival in St. Petersburg. Though Japan had never officially declared her intention of opening up negotiations for an agreement with Russia, her actions during the past year had naturally induced Russia to anticipate negotiations. The failure to realize these anticipations must certainly have caused Russia to resent deeply the alliance, and, indeed, to resent the whole Japanese attitude, assuming that that country had insulted her with a lie. Being a great country she naturally did not publicly display this feeling, but undoubtedly

the Russian dislike of Japan deepened more
and more.

The statements made by M. Kurino to the
authorities in Paris, previous to his learning
of the Anglo-Japanese negotiations from Baron
Tsusuki, must also have been transmitted by
her ally to Russia. The result of this must
have been to convince the St. Petersburg
authorities either that the new Japanese
Minister was a person with an extraordinary
capacity for intrigue or that he was entirely
unreliable and even uninformed as to his own
Government's intentions and policy.

Anyhow, the Anglo-Japanese negotiations
had reached by that time such a point that
their suspension would have meant a loss of
confidence throughout the world.

By the alliance the confidence of Russia
and France in Japan was diminished to a
considerable extent. She was discredited by
them.

Even in the most critical moments of a
country's history it is most important to
maintain the confidence reposed in a country
by friendly Powers. In international relations faith is the most essential element.

The principles of the Anglo-Japanese Alliance were decided in August, 1901; the negotiations were already commenced when in

September negotiations were put forward to Russia, Japan's erstwhile enemy, with a view to the conclusion of a Russo-Japanese Agreement. The danger of such a course lay not only in the loss of confidence abroad in Japan, but in the risk of wrecking the negotiations with England. Fortunately these latter had practically come to a close before the overtures to Russia had resulted in anything serious. But, suppose Marquis Ito had not delayed so long in, and on his way from America, what would have been the result? Or suppose the Russian negotiations had been conducted in Japan, instead of in St. Petersburg! Then certainly Japan would have lost the confidence of both the great Powers (England and Russia). It is horrible even to think of what might have happened.

In reference to the relations of the alliance with Germany, it is desirable to say something more. After my first conversations with Baron Eckardstein, the Councillor of the German Embassy in London, he never referred to the matter again. On our side we felt under no necessity to induce Germany to participate in the alliance, and consequently we never invited Germany to come in. Of course if such a step had been suggested from the German side, it would have been a differ-

ent matter. Owing to the subsequent un-
pleasant relations between Great Britain and
Germany, no inducement was offered to
Germany from that side either.

Having regard to the circumstances which
then existed, and in particular the relations
between Germany and Russia, it is plain that
Germany never seriously thought of participating in the treaty. This was clearly shown
by the German declaration excluding the
whole of Manchuria from the scope of the
Anglo-German Agreement, a course Germany
took soon after the conclusion of that convention.

The editor of a certain influential magazine
in London wrote to me saying that Baron
Eckardstein claimed that the British and
Japanese Governments had of *malice prepense*
excluded Germany from participation. But
really what I have said about the origins of
the alliance testifies that if Germany had
wanted to join the alliance she would have
been admitted. From the outset, however,
nothing was proposed by Germany nor was
any wish to join expressed by her.

Naturally, as the result of the subsequent
victory of Japan over Russia, Germany must
have felt more or less inconvenience in the
Far East, even though the exposure of Russian

weakness might have been a great satisfaction in other ways. The recent successes of German policy in the Balkans has probably been a consequence of this exposure.

In the present day, now that the Russo-Japanese War has been so happily terminated and the Second Alliance Treaty has been concluded, no one in Japan would dream of opposing the alliance.

The Anglo-Japanese Alliance is the established policy of Japan. It is the basis of the country's foreign policy. It was concluded owing to the common interests of the two countries demanding it, a demand supported by the traditional relations of the two countries. The alliance may, therefore, be regarded as resting on the most solid foundation. Every effort and every mischievous trick having for its object the splitting of the tie cementing the two countries must end in failure.

My story of the alliance is now finished, and in other chapters I will treat of other ancient histories. Before actually concluding this chapter, however, I will pen the following incident, which is not without much interest.

On January 8th of this year a certain Fukushima contributed an article to the *Hochi*

Shimbun (organ of Count Okuma), entitled "A Reminiscence of the Chounkaku," claiming that it was told him by Marquis Katsura.

It ran as follows: "Origin of the Anglo-Japanese Alliance. It was a very hot day (August 4th) in 1901, when Prince (then Marquis) Ito arrived here (Chounkaku, Marquis Katsura's villa) from Kanazawa, Prince (then Marquis) Yamagata from Oiso, Marquis (then Count) Inouye from Okitsu, and Marquis (then Count) Matsukata from Kamakura, and in this very room conferred on the proposed alliance, the necessity for which was deeply felt. These statesmen fell to discussion of the clauses of the Alliance Treaty and other matters. So was the alliance truly originated. At that moment Marquis Ito took his 'fudo' (pen brush) and wrote on this 'kakemono,' naming the house 'Chounkaku' or 'dome of a long cloud.' This Council was quite unknown to the public, as all the statesmen assembled here from their respective country villas, and this house is quite distant from Tokio."

The Opinion for a Russo-Japanese Alliance.

"Subsequently Marquis Ito proceeded to Europe and returned to Japan after visiting

Russia. After his return he maintained an opinion that a Russo-Japanese Alliance was necessary. If Prince Ito had been in power it might have been necessary to regard such an alliance as essential. But the relations between Japan and Russia were steadily worsening, and it was clear that the situation might sooner or later culminate in a war. Besides, the negotiations with Great Britain had reached a point at which the clauses had been drafted, whilst the idea of a Russian Alliance, as Marquis Ito desired, had not even got so far as being officially approved. The Marquis, however, pressed his views so insistently that we were finally compelled absolutely to reject the proposal. However, Marquis Ito ever after appeared to entertain great displeasure about it.

"The result of the conference at the Choun-kaku on August 4th was reported to Count Hayashi by telegram on August 8th."

In spite of the statement credited to the Premier, Count Katsura, that the public was then ignorant of the conference, I, as has already been related, was informed about the conference. If Count Katsura had made up his mind for the Anglo-Japanese Alliance at that time it is incomprehensible to me how he could have dispatched Marquis Ito to

14

Russia and thus run a great risk of rupturing the negotiations with England. It is incredible that Ito agreed to the proposed alliance at the Chounkaku and afterwards proceeded to Russia to open negotiations without having a previous agreement with the Premier. Even admitting that Ito went to Russia on his own initiative, he could not have entered into formal negotiations with Russia without the Premier's approval. This hypothesis must, therefore, be excluded from consideration. It is clear that the Premier, on the one hand, decided to negotiate an alliance with Great Britain, and, on the other, dispatched Marquis Ito to Russia to negotiate an agreement, and in so doing dangerously risked the credit of the State.

With regard to the statement in the *Hochi Shimbun* that after Ito's return from Europe he still held out stoutly for a Russian Alliance, it is to be noted that the alliance was published on February 12, 1902. According to a report which I subsequently received from Mr. Hisamizu, I.J. Consul at Singapore, Marquis Ito arrived at that port on that date. The Consul immediately went aboard to pay his respects to the Marquis and took with him a clipping from the local paper reproducing the text of the alliance, and congratulated the Marquis

Photo   Nadar, Paris

THE LATE PRINCE HIROBUMI ITO

JAPAN'S GREATEST STATESMAN, ASSASSINATED BY A KOREAN FANATIC,
OCTOBER 26TH, 1909

on its conclusion. Anyhow, the alliance was signed long before the Marquis arrived back in Japan from Europe. Even if on his return he had been ignorant that the alliance had been actually signed I cannot believe that he would have still pressed for an alliance with Russia.

The "Reminiscence" which I have quoted from the *Hochi Shimbun* contains a good deal more about the Anglo-Japanese Alliance, but much of what is related is contradictory to the facts and entirely at variance with the official documents. Such statements as that attributed to Marquis Katsura are confused and wrong. As the Premier was not the sort of man to circulate baseless utterances through the Press, it may be that the printers have made many mistakes.[1]

[1] The only portion of the "Reminiscence" from the *Hochi Shimbun,* quoted above, which does not tally is the statement that Ito, on his return from Europe, still pressed for a Russian Alliance. If the "Reminiscence" read, "Ito after leaving St. Petersburg still pressed for a Russian Alliance," the facts would be truly represented, for as Count Hayashi himself relates, he did this both directly to Hayashi and through Matsui at Berlin and at Tokio through Marquis Inouye. When Ito arrived back the Cabinet were so afraid of his criticism that M. Kato was sent to Nagasaki to appease him.—ED.

CHAPTER VI

The Franco-Japanese Agreement

THE Franco-Japanese Agreement had its origin in Paris. I have in the chapter dealing with the Anglo-Japanese Alliance related that M. Kurino, formerly the Japanese Minister in Paris, and later in St. Petersburg, was a person of marked pro-French sentiment, and there were also at that time in France many important people of pro-Japanese sentiment. Amongst the most noteworthy of these were M. Lanessan, who had formerly held the post of Governor-General of Annam and Cochin-China and later the post of Minister of Marine. He was one of the most earnest advocates of a Franco-Japanese *rapprochement*.

As has been related earlier, M. Kurino[1] and other persons who held the same view

---

[1] Kurino, Viscount Shin-ichiro, b. 1852. Minister at Washington, 1894; at Rome, 1896; at Paris, 1897; at St. Petersburg, 1901 until February, 1904; at Paris, 1906–1912.

as he did expected at first to sign a Franco-
Japanese Treaty. But the negotiations between Great Britain and Japan having
culminated in an Anglo-Japanese Alliance
the proposals for an arrangement with France
fell into the background.

Then followed the Russo-Japanese War,
which was itself followed by an Anglo-French
rapprochement. As the result of the Treaty
of Portsmouth the last barriers to a Franco-
Japanese entente were removed, and ideas
with regard to a formal convention were
revived.

In general the French people were friendly
to Japan, but as the result of the Russo-
Japanese War and the previous incidents of
the three-Power intervention with regard to
the retrocession of Port Arthur, and owing
to the close relations which existed between
France and Russia, which resulted in the
flagrant disregard of international law and
neutrality by France in regard to her actions
at Madagascar and Kamranh Bay, the idea
was prevalent in France that although the
French were in themselves amicably inclined
to Japan, yet the Japanese were not desirous
of being friendly to France. The majority
of French people believed that the Japanese
deeply resented the French course of action,

and were sincerely afraid that one day the French colonies in Annam would be attacked by the Japanese. There is good reason to believe that the breach of neutrality committed by the French during the war might have seriously affected the feelings of the Japanese people, and if the Japanese had been defeated in the naval battle of the Straits of Tsushima then indeed the Japanese hostility towards the French would have been a permanent one. As things turned out, however, the Japanese victory was overwhelming, and the excitement and satisfaction of the Japanese nation entirely overshadowed any resentment they felt against France on account of the breaches of neutrality. In their triumph after the war they entirely forgot the affair.

At the time when the idea was revived in Japan for an agreement with France to be made, the French people still felt considerable anxiety on the point. Such being the circumstances, pro-Japanese Frenchmen and pro-French Japanese made considerable exertions to try to remove the barriers and misunderstandings which existed between the two countries, and as the result their endeavours were crowned by the successful negotiation of the Franco-Japanese Agreement.

The True Significance of the Convention.

Apparently the agreement seems to have no especial significance, but if it has been closely watched it will have been seen that Japan has for instance commercial relations with the province of Fukien, which is situated on the mainland opposite to the island of Formosa. Japanese influence in that province dates from the time when the Japanese occupied the island of Formosa, which was formerly attached to the province of Fukien.

The inhabitants of Formosa are mostly Chinese originally from Fukien, and they maintain the most intimate connexion between the island and the mainland, and in case of trouble in Fukien steps would at once have to be taken to prevent the disturbances overflowing to the island and affecting its inhabitants.

Quite similar conditions might be anticipated in the neighbourhood of Annam, and consequently it was a matter of the utmost importance and of great mutual benefit that France and Japan should take steps to avoid as far as possible incurring trouble such as I have suggested. There is, however, no intention nor idea, as has been suggested, that the one country should lend military aid to the other in case of necessity.

The "open door and equal opportunity" are quite ordinary principles, but where special relations and special interests exist then other means have to be considered. Great Britain was the first to realize this, and for a long time she paid very special attention to the protection of her special interests in the Yangtse Valley, in Canton, and in Kowloon. Similar efforts have been made by Germany in Shantung in the neighbourhood of the leased territory of Kiaochow.

Logically speaking, there is no special sphere of influence created in either case, but in principle special efforts have been made to protect and safeguard the points of greatest interest to the nation in question.

In the preamble of the Franco-Japanese Treaty only the principle of the open door is mentioned, but in the succeeding articles something which very much resembles the significance of the sphere of influence is to be found. The introduction of this caused very great difficulties in the drafting of the treaty.

As the Chinese were more closely interested in the treaty than the Japanese they naturally gave much more careful consideration to the wording of the treaty.

At the time of its publication the vernacular papers in Shanghai made various comments on the treaty, but as a matter of fact there was no special meaning latent behind the wording of the published article guaranteeing the peace and safety of the parts neighbouring on the territories of the high contracting parties. The whole policy of the Franco-Japanese Treaty did in fact aim at the avoidance of all trouble in the provinces neighbouring on the French and Japanese possessions.

There is no reason whatsoever for any fear from the side of the Chinese. In certain cases of comment on the Japanese side it was claimed that the sphere of influence was restricted, and a certain Japanese who spoke to me on the matter said that the treaty would not prove so simple a one as it looked.

Another advantage which we have gained by it is an improvement of our commercial position in Annam. Before the treaty was signed the Japanese were not very favourably considered in that country, but by virtue of the declaration attached to the treaty they will be able to receive the most favourable nation treatment, and obtain thereby very considerable benefits.

In addition to the above advantage, the treaty has already had and will continue to have good fruit in dissipating the suspicions of the French people. Already we have experienced material benefits from it in connexion with the floating of Japanese bonds on the French market.

In reference to the conclusion of the treaty I may admit that it was most earnestly advocated by Marquis Inouye, whilst Princes Ito and Yamagata and Marquis Katsura gave it strong support. In fact, these statesmen were consistently consulted on phases of its policy by the late (Saionji) Cabinet, and therefore the present (Katsura) Cabinet has no good grounds for attacking its predecessor.

The treaty with France was signed on June 10, 1907.

NOTE.—The text of the Franco-Japanese Agreement will be found in Appendix C.

The Franco-Japanese Agreement is worth a good deal more attention than Count Hayashi gives it in his *Memoirs*, although, reading between the lines, the reasons for his somewhat curt dismissal of it are fairly obvious. In his statement the Count puts on record that the Japanese Foreign Office, whilst openly supposed to be supporting the policy of the open door, was in fact maintaining the old policy of the "sphere of influence." In doing so the Count entirely substantiates the charges of bad faith that have again and again been brought against the Japanese Foreign Office by all classes trading in China, and especially with Manchuria and parts where Japan has obtained a special hold.

The Franco-Japanese Agreement, looked at from another point of view, was a natural corollary of the Anglo-Japanese Alliance and a complement of the Russo-Japanese Convention, signed in the same year. These three agreements practically closed the ring round China for the exclusive benefit of what has been described as the China Pooling Syndicate. This consisted of Great Britain, Japan, Russia, and France, and excluded Germany and the United States. Nevertheless, highly satisfied as Count Hayashi was with the result of his labours and confident as he was of the approval the agreement should receive, it did not in fact find as warm a welcome as he hoped. In Japan a considerable party, unfavourably inclined to the general policy of the Cabinet, considered it not only as superfluous, but as actually introducing into the China situation a fourth party, whose interests had hitherto been looked after by Russia. A writer in *Kokumin Shimbun*, the organ of the Katsura faction, said: "France is not nearly so interested in China as Japan, yet the new treaty elevates her to an equal position with Japan as a guardian of the integrity of China."

The *Spectator*, in a long and truly remarkable criticism, which is quoted at length by Mr. Putnam Weale in *The Coming Struggle in Eastern Asia*, pointed out that a ring composed of Britain, France, Russia, and Japan to control China, would prove ineffective so long as Germany and America were excluded. The weekly review pointed out that Japan's policy of ignoring Germany and keeping that country outside the charmed circle was wrong and stupid. "China," said the writer of the article, "interests the traders of Berlin as much as those of London. If the other Powers deliberately excluded Germany it was not impossible that that country might find the means of posing to China as a disinterested adviser. When Germany holds aloof from any great arrangement the arrangement can hardly be accepted as being final."

Those who followed the Quintuple Loan negotiations in Peking will realize that this prophecy was then fulfilled. Even to-day, in spite of the fall of Tsingtau, Germany is more respected in Peking than any other European Power, because she was the only one which appeared to have no political axe to grind as the price of her participation in the loan. It will be an interesting study for the historian of the future to resolve to what extent German dislike of Great Britain has been due to her considered exclusion from the international agreements intended to settle the fate of China. It does not make very much difference to the problem that these agreements, as the Revolution has shown, have but little real influence on the ultimate fate of the country. The exclusion of the United States referred to in the article quoted was to some extent remedied by the Root-Takahira Agreement mentioned in another chapter.

The policy advocated by the *Spectator* was as ill-advised as that which it condemned. It was simply to get all the Powers without exception into a ring and then to force China to accept the domination of the West, whatsoever form it might take. The very idea of dominating a nation of 400,000,000 is humorous. A Mohammedan is reported to have once said to an Indian official: "If we were really to rise against the British we should only have to throw our turbans on top of you to stifle you all." When the Chinese Revolution broke out in 1911 the writer was on his way to the Far East. A missionary in the train said: "Well, if they really rise against the foreigners and only march on us with sticks in their hands, no power on earth could save us."

The Chinese vernacular Press was able to see behind the wording of the treaty as clearly as its author. To them it was nothing but a revival of the spheres of influence and of the policy of grab. The following passage from the *Nan Fang Pao* is eloquent of distrust and disgust: "The publication of the text of the Franco-Japanese Agreement has naturally created a stir in the Chinese world, but the effect produced, if the pronouncements of the Chinese Press are any indication, is quite the reverse of that on foreigners, as expressed by the tone of the British Press. Our newspapers can see nothing to congratulate China on in the agreement, and cannot say with any show of unction that the integrity of our country is more strongly assured by the consummation of the entente or that the peace of the Far East is rendered more secure.

"Nearly all the papers realize the importance of the agreement in its effect on China, though that such an agreement could be effected at all came somewhat as a surprise to them. The traditional and innate contempt of the white race for the yellow race would seem to be an insurmountable obstacle to bring about any understanding; and the world is now treated to the spectacle of first an Anglo-Japanese Alliance and now a Franco-Japanese Agreement—an agreement which further receives the moral support of Great Britain and Russia. By the conclusion of the agreement, two nations, if we exclude the contracting parties, are directly or indirectly affected by it, namely, Germany and China. The former is made to feel her isolated position, while the interests of the latter are placed in greater jeopardy than before.

"What strikes the Chinese Press as somewhat meaningless is the eternal reiteration on the part of certain Powers of their intention to respect the independence and integrity of China. As one of the papers said, such a settlement can only tickle the ears of our effete and blind Government, but it has not a sufficient ring of sincerity about it to deceive the people. By the terms of the agreement the influence of Japan and of France in the Chinese Empire is greatly strengthened. Whatever has been leased by the Chinese Government is now almost invested with the rights of occupation, and whatever has not been leased, but is bordering on the leased territory, is in danger of being enclosed in the same.

"After the Chino-Japanese War the Japanese sphere of influence in China was confined to the Province of Fukien, and now we are informed that on account of the Japanese interests in the Liaotung Peninsula both Chihli and Shantung have been included. The sphere of France is also greatly extended by the terms of this agreement. At first it was only her vague ambitions that the provinces of Yunnan, Kuangtung, and Kuangsi, should be her share in the despoiling of China, but in the past few years we have seen the gradual growth of her ambition, till now the provinces are to become in reality the reward of her many years of scheming. It is to be noted that the tactics of France and Japan in their undermining of China's integrity and independence have been almost identical. The former first detached Annam from China's suzerainty, then seized the region itself, and gradually encroached on the borders of Yunnan and the two Kuangs till now she is stretching her arms even to the interior of those provinces; while with Japan Korea was her first object, from which she directed her attention to Manchuria, and now Chihli and Shantung are to be enclosed within her grasp.

"The Anglo-Japanese Alliance was claimed to be concluded to preserve the peace of the Far East, but the devastated condition of Manchuria bears eloquent witness to the validity or otherwise of the claim. Let us hope and pray that the Franco-Japanese Agreement, which starts out with language of similar strain of function, may not end as disastrously for our Empire."

With the above may be compared the following passage from the *Memoirs of Li Hung-Chang* (Foster):

"Foreigners say that they lease our lands. We know that they are gone for ever."—Ed.

CHAPTER VII
The Russo-Japanese Convention
1907

LAST year when the Saionji Cabinet collapsed and the present second Katsura Cabinet was formed, financial re-adjustment and the improvement of our foreign policy were declared to be the principal planks in the platform of the new Ministry. These two reforms which we, the Saionji Cabinet, were declared to have essayed so badly, will only be properly carried through by the successes which we attained.

At the time that the Budget of 1908–1909 was formulated the ex-Premier Marquis Katsura was closely consulted by the Ministry, and to a certain extent he was morally responsible for that Budget.

With regard to the Budget of 1909–1910, the Saionji Cabinet had fallen before any steps were taken to prepare it, and as a consequence is in no way responsible for any part of it. It was drawn up by the present Cabinet, who alone are answerable for its unexpected and unsatisfactory nature. We could certainly have drawn up as good a Budget and perhaps a better one.

As financial matters were not under my control when I was a Minister of State, and as, further, I am not well acquainted with matters of finance, I had to content myself with the explanations offered to the Cabinet by the Minister of Finance, and as long as those explanations seemed satisfactory to the Cabinet I gave my approval also.

I do not think, however, that such a condition of affairs is very satisfactory. The financial policy of the Government must affect very closely the foreign policy. The financial policy of a country, especially if it is a creditor country, directly affects foreign countries. The Minister of Finance ought, therefore, to be a real financial expert, capable of properly explaining the true conditions of Japanese finances, so as to carry weight with the investing public, both Japanese and foreign. With regard to foreign affairs, I would even go so far as to advocate a similar course being adopted.

I held in the Saionji Cabinet the responsible

position of Minister of Foreign Affairs, and on account of holding that important portfolio I was compelled to refrain from public utterances and from comment on current events. Now, however, I have been relieved from my post as a Minister I believe that the time has come for me to review the charges brought against Marquis Saionji's Ministry with regard to its management of foreign affairs.

It is natural that as the present Ministry has attacked our so-called diplomatic inactivity one should hear occasionally from Marquis Katsura complaints on the same score. Two or three newspapers, taking their cue from the Ministerial party, have also attacked us. The object, however, of the different papers varies. Some newspapers attack any Government indiscriminately, and for the reason that they are always against the Government have attacked us also. Other papers seem to have a more definite motive and confine their criticism to definite· points, as China.

The public in Japan is rather cool in its interest in foreign affairs, indeed I could almost say that it is indifferent. When, however, something happens that forces the public to pay some attention to foreign affairs, then at once the public seems to get intoxicated, as though drunk with alcohol, and it behaves as if it were not able to discriminate, just as an intoxicated person cannot tell the difference between *sake* and water.

In just the same manner the public, when its interest is awakened on matters of foreign policy, is totally unable to discriminate between diplomatic activity and diplomatic inactivity. Directly someone raises a charge against the Ministry of Foreign Affairs, the public commences a virulent attack on the Ministry for what it calls diplomatic inactivity, and amongst the accusers may even be found many members of Parliament, who ought to know better. And, in addition, many people who really know the true conditions of affairs are inclined to hold back for private reasons, when by stating the truth they could assist the Ministry.

It would be childish to deal with the irrational and indiscriminate attacks of which there have been many. Against these it is better to maintain a dignified silence. But even irrational attacks, if originated for purposes of effecting a Ministerial change, must be dealt with and answered if only for the reasons of self-defence.

The most important items of the late

Cabinet's foreign policy which were the subjects of bitter attacks were the Russo-Japanese Convention, the Russian commercial and fishery questions, the Franco-Japanese Agreement, as well as the less definite question of the Japanese post-bellum policy in Manchuria, Japanese policy in China and Korea, and the American immigration question.

With regard to these various matters a distinction should be drawn between those for the settlement of which both the late Saionji and the present Katsura Cabinets were jointly responsible, and those for which we alone were responsible. If this distinction is properly drawn it will at once be seen that the attacks of the present Ministry on its predecessors are rational or irrational according as the late Ministry was or was not alone answerable for each subject of attack.

To draw such a distinction is also desirable for the disarmament of the hasty critics of foreign affairs, and also to give some encouragement towards the proper study of foreign affairs by the public at large. If the result of answering the charges which have been made against us, many of them absurd, is to stop further irresponsible criticism of a Government, then much good will have been done and the free action of diplomacy in the future will have been much facilitated.

I intend to treat of the post-bellum policy of Japan in Manchuria and China in a following chapter. But I have a special reason for making this statement now, because the venom of the Katsura attack on us has been concentrated on our post-bellum conduct in China rather than on the Russo-Japanese Commercial and Fishery Conventions, although in those conventions we made more or less concessions to the other side. The reason why the Katsura party has carefully avoided the Russian Conventions is because they were provided for in the Treaty of Portsmouth and were the natural outcome of that treaty. Consequently, the persons who were responsible for that treaty could not possibly attack the supplementary treaties, which were so necessary to complete the work which they had commenced.

Certainly minor points might give rise to discussion, but in concluding treaties mutual concessions are necessary in order to arrive at a result that is agreeable to both sides.

A great Italian statesman once said that the only satisfactory treaty would be one which should be unsatisfactory to everybody concerned.

Even granting that our new treaties with Russia contain some imperfect points, that is not a sufficient reason to condemn us for this so-called diplomatic inactivity. As a matter of fact, in all the attacks which have been made on us no one has claimed that any clause of those treaties is unfavourable. It may, therefore, be presumed that they are satisfactory.

With regard to the Russo-Japanese Agreement, this was the result of the imperfections of the Treaty of Portsmouth, which was concluded by the first Katsura Cabinet. In my opinion the present Cabinet, in attacking our conclusion of the convention, is entirely lacking in discrimination of the rights and privileges of the two contracting parties. The agreement was really only a corollary to the Treaty of Portsmouth, which was made by the first Katsura Ministry. Although a great deal of criticism has been published about the unsatisfactory conditions of peace signed at Portsmouth, those who know the real circumstances recognize that at the time the negotiations were in progress it was abolutely necessary for us to make peace.

There were similar reasons for the conclusion of the convention under discussion, and it is in such circumstances, when explanations to the public are obviously impossible, that diplomatists find themselves in the greatest embarrassment.

Of course the negotiations between Russia and Japan at Portsmouth cannot be compared with, for example, the negotiations between Germany and France for the capitulation of Paris. The circumstances were very different.

It was absolutely impossible for any one who knew the real facts of the internal conditions and of the military situation to expect us to reap much advantage from the Treaty of Portsmouth. It was natural that that treaty should have many imperfections.

Knowing the true facts and then recalling the famous Hibiya Park disturbances, one cannot but consider these latter as an overwhelming proof of the rudimentary state of the Japanese mind in relation to foreign affairs.

One must admit, of course, that the Treaty of Portsmouth, although it ended the war with Russia, was from the Japanese point of view insufficient and unsatisfactory. It was owing to their recognition of this that Prince Yamagata and Prince Ito, as soon as the treaty had been concluded, commenced working for the conclusion of a Russo-Japanese Convention which should supplement the Treaty of Portsmouth.

In the beginning of 1907, Dr. Dillon contributed two articles to reviews in England, urging the necessity of a Russo-Japanese *rapprochement*. These articles were shown to M. Motono, our Ambassador at St. Petersburg, by M. Iswolsky, who was at that time the Russian Minister for Foreign Affairs. These articles were evidently written after conversation with some high person in the Russian Government, and M. Motono believed that they indicated the undoubted intention of the Russian Government of entering into an agreement with Japan on the lines laid down in the articles. M. Motono drew the attention of the Japanese Foreign Office to the articles and asked for an opinion on them.

I should say something about Dr. Dillon. His father was an Englishman and his mother was Irish. He was educated at various continental universities and he possessed several high diplomas of learning. For some time he was professor at various Russian universities and also had been the proprietor of a newspaper at Odessa.

He married a Russian lady and resided in St. Petersburg. At the time that I was Minister and Ambassador in London, Dr. Dillon was the St. Petersburg correspondent of the *Daily Telegraph*, and probably is so to-day. He certainly was most extraordinarily well acquainted with all Russian affairs, and any statement made by him in the *Daily Telegraph* having reference to Russia was always regarded as being based on the highest authority.

I met him two or three times whilst I was in London. When Count de Witte proceeded to America as the chief Russian plenipotentiary to negotiate the terms of peace at Portsmouth, Dr. Dillon paid me a visit in London and I had a long conversation with him on various subjects. The principal object of his visit to me was to request me to do everything which I could to induce the Japanese Government to dispatch Marquis Ito to America as the principal Japanese Peace Commissioner.

When the negotiations were proceeding at Portsmouth it was Dr. Dillon who controlled the American Press for the benefit of de Witte. At that time most of the prominent British and American correspondents who had collected at Portsmouth had gone there inclined to be in favour of Japan.

Dr. Dillon used these men to publish the real existing state of affairs without any reserve whatsoever, and was unrivalled by anybody on the Japanese side in creating a favourable public opinion. He did it almost entirely by relying on the influence of the American papers, to whose correspondents at Portsmouth he always stated the exact position of affairs. On the Japanese side, on the other hand, nothing was done like this. True, there was a member of the Japanese Foreign Office staff attached to the Peace Commission, and it was supposed to be his duty to receive the newspaper men. In fact he had nothing else to do but that. But he made his principal task the denying of every statement which might appear.

In view of my experience in diplomacy I considered that such a course was a matter of the greatest regret. Comparing the action of the two sides at Portsmouth as regards the Press, it was only natural that the umpire's fan was pointed at Japan from the very outset of the negotiations, and she was never able to recover from the unsatisfactory Press position into which she allowed herself to fall, a position which was principally due to the fact that the Japanese authorities preserved far too much silence as to the progress of the negotiations.

With regard to the Russo-Japanese Agreement,[1] about which I commenced to speak, Prince Yamagata and Prince Ito, as well as

[1] For text see Appendix D.

M. Iswolsky, recognized the absolute necessity of concluding an agreement such as had been outlined by Dr. Dillon in his articles to which I have referred.

A conference was held with the principal members of the previous Cabinet and no objection was raised on their side to the proposal. Instructions were, therefore, given to M. Motono to sound the Russian Government and find out if it were seriously desirous of making an agreement. When he reported that this was the case I telegraphed him formal power to negotiate a convention. From the very beginning there was no hitch, and the negotiations made such steady progress that the agreement was signed on July 30, 1907.

In reference to this agreement conferences were held from time to time with the Elder Statesmen, and Prince Katsura attended these meetings and never once raised any opposition to the proposed convention.

Prince Yamagata interested himself very deeply in the matter and expressed himself with the deepest satisfaction when it had been successfully concluded. In fact, it was said that Prince Yamagata felt as proud of the agreement as if he alone had had the merit of concluding it.

Although Marquis Katsura did not express

such deep satisfaction he never showed any
opposition to it, and there is no reason why
his Cabinet should now attack it or us, unless
a certain report that he considered the agreement to be a reflection on his conduct of the
war and peace may be credible.

NOTE.—The Russo-Japanese Convention, which,
like the Franco-Japanese Convention, was a platitudin-
ous instrument supposed to ensure the maintenance
of the status in the Far East, had been preceded in
the previous month by the conclusion of the railway
and other Russo-Japanese Conventions stipulated in
the Treaty of Portsmouth.

The convention itself, on the Russian side at least,
does not appear to have been considered as more
than a piece of diplomatic courtesy. On the Japanese side it was intimately connected with internal
politics. The first Saionji Cabinet was only a make-
shift affair. Almost from the day of its appointment
it was the object of severe criticism, especially from
the military party, which was strongly opposed to the
evacuation of Manchuria, and which did actually
succeed in prolonging the same for about a year
beyond the agreed date. Principally owing to Count
Hayashi, the Cabinet was in constant conflict with
the army, not that the Count was opposed to the goal
aimed at by the soldiers, namely, the permanent
occupation of Manchuria, but because he realized
what a serious loss of credit would accrue to Japan by
failure to implement such an important condition
of the peace terms.

The mistake which Count Hayashi seems to have

made was in thinking that because the Saionji Cabinet was in power that it was, therefore, going to govern the country. The policies of Japan are made by the Genro and merely executed by the Ministry for the time being. With a majority of the Genro belonging to the militarist faction it is easy to realize the difficult position in which a Minister bent on curbing the ambitions of the army would find himself.

The Saionji Cabinet got enough rope to hang itself, and then Marquis Katsura came back to power.

Although from time to time the *Gwaimusho* referred to the Russo-Japanese Convention as one of the instruments on which the peace of the Extreme Orient hinged, it was generally considered in diplomatic circles as being unimportant. It has since been amply proved to have been merely the vain repetition of phrases in which neither side had any trust. Count Hayashi was undoubtedly glad to negotiate it as something to put forward in the Diet in answer to the inevitable bogey of every Japanese Foreign Minister, the charge of a "negative" policy. It would have been of considerable importance if the treaties, conventions, and contracts with China, mentioned in the instrument, had been attached and published. In that case it would have been good evidence whether Russia was at the back of Japan in connexion with the Fa-ku-men Railway affair and also whether it was on this occasion that Russia and Japan agreed on that extraordinary interpretation of the Chinese Eastern Railway Agreement which gave the two Powers administrative rights over the settlements along the line to the abrogation of Chinese sovereignty. On neither of these two points does Count Hayashi say anything, so that one is forced to the deduction that they were not discussed, as otherwise he could not have restrained himself from displaying such a considerable diplomatic success as agreement on these points would have been. As regulating the Far Eastern relations of Japan and Russia, the 1907 Agreement has been completely displaced by the 1910 Convention and subsequent unpublished but well-known instruments.—ED.

CHAPTER VIII

The American-Japanese Agreement
1908

[The Agreement was in reality an exchange of notes
between Mr. Elihu Root and M. Takahira, Imperial
Japanese Ambassador at Washington.[1]—Ed.]

THE next matter which I want to consider
is the convention or agreement made between
Japan and America in 1908, by the second
Katsura Cabinet.

This convention had been proposed to the
previous Cabinet (the first Saionji Cabinet)
by Viscount Aoki, the Japanese Ambassador
at Washington. The Saionji Cabinet had
not, however, approved of the conclusion of
the proposed agreement, but it has suddenly
been concluded by the present Cabinet (the
second Katsura Cabinet).

From the point of view of the statesman
now in power (Prince Katsura), the signature

[1] See Appendix E.

239

of the agreement with America might be regarded as a diplomatic success and as an indication of the renewal of energy in our foreign policy, in contra-distinction to what people describe as the diplomatic inactivity of the last (Saionji) Cabinet.

No doubt the present Cabinet has had good reasons for signing the agreement, but equally without doubt the late Cabinet had good reasons for regarding the agreement as unnecessary. Further, there is good proof that the present Premier (Prince Katsura) recognized as proper the reasons of his predecessor for refusing to consent to the agreement, and consequently it is improper for him now to claim that our failure to conclude the agreement was due to diplomatic inactivity.

Likewise it is premature to contend that the conclusion of the agreement is due to a renewal of energy in our foreign affairs. It would be fairer to let readers draw their own conclusions from the facts.

Towards the close of the spring of 1907, Viscount Aoki, Japanese Ambassador at Washington, suddenly dispatched a telegram to the Foreign Minister at Tokio (myself) reporting that he, in his individual capacity, had suggested an Americo-Japanese Treaty to the President of the United States (Mr.

Roosevelt), who had accepted the suggestion. He reported further the terms of the proposed convention, which were identical with those of the diplomatic *communiqué* of 1906. The President had agreed to these terms.

When this telegram was received at the Foreign Office, the opinion was firmly held that such conditions as those proposed, namely, to respect the mutual privileges of friendly Powers, ought to be regarded as the ordinary etiquette of international affairs. As to concluding special conventions amongst all the Powers to ensure such respect, there would never be time enough, even if it were a necessity.

Moreover, there was no question likely to arise which could impair the friendship between America and Japan, except the immigration question—and our Ambassador added in his telegram that he had specifically omitted the immigration question from the treaty.

In such case Viscount Aoki's proposed treaty could only be regarded as superfluous. And if it were concluded it would only arouse suspicion that some question had existed of a nature to cause friction between the two countries, and necessitating the conclusion of a treaty which otherwise would have been without a definite object.

16

An opinion of this tenor was drawn up and presented to the Cabinet by the Foreign Office, and approved by the Cabinet.

At the same time, however, a copy of Viscount Aoki's telegram was transmitted to Prince Ito, at that time Imperial Japanese Resident-General in Seoul (Korea). It happened that Prince Katsura was also at the moment in Seoul, and the two entered into a minute discussion of Japan's diplomacy towards America. They condemned the attempt made by Viscount Aoki to carry on diplomatic negotiations without having first either learned the intentions or obtained the consent of his Government. They said that a hundred such declarations (as that proposed) would be "vain letters" without a solution of the labour and immigration questions, which would remain obstacles to Japanese friendship with America. The opinions of Princes Ito and Katsura coincided with that of the Foreign Office and of the Cabinet.

So it is clear that whatever different reason the present Cabinet may have had for concluding the treaty, the failure of the late Cabinet to conclude it cannot be alleged to be a sign of diplomatic inactivity.

It is a diplomatic usage to believe that if an Ambassador in his private capacity puts forward a proposal to the Government to which he is accredited, he is sounding the intentions of that Government, acting on the instructions of his own. In the event of the Government to which he is accredited disagreeing with the views set out in his proposal, it can decline the same without in any way injuring the feelings of the proposer. Or he can withdraw his proposal without affecting the dignity of his own Government.

But if an Ambassador puts forward on his own initiative, even in his private capacity, a proposal without having learnt the views of his Government, and this proposal is accepted by the party to whom it is offered, but rejected by the Ambassador's Government, serious consequences will result. The home Government has taken into consideration matters not within the purview of the Ambassador, and cannot approve of such Ambassadorial proposals. Otherwise the Ambassador would seem to be Foreign Minister and the Foreign Minister would be taking his instructions from the Ambassador.

If a Government is in the position of having to disapprove of a proposal put forward by its Ambassador, in the manner described, the foreign Government concerned can no longer repose confidence in any statement emanating from that Ambassador, with the result that both the dignity of that Government and the confidence in that Ambassador must be injured.

In ancient days, when the means of communication were less perfect, Ministers abroad necessarily had often to act arbitrarily. In the present day the least event in Eastern Asia penetrates to the furthest corners of Europe and America. With the modern inventions in telegraphy, Ministers stationed abroad can easily avoid all risks of impairing the friendly feelings between States. There is no longer necessity for them to risk a loss of confidence by arbitrary action on their own parts.

The text of the treaty concluded by the present Cabinet closely resembles the draft prepared by Viscount Aoki when Ambassador at Washington under the preceding Cabinet. What was the reason which made Prince Katsura regard its conclusion as a necessity, when last year he opposed it, is unknown. It is clear, however, from the statements of the American Press, that the conclusion of the treaty had far less influence in affecting American sentiment towards Japan and creating a pro-Japanese feeling in America than the receptions accorded to the American Fleet and the American Business Men's Delegation.

As a matter of fact, both these receptions had been arranged by the Saionji Cabinet, although they actually matured under its successor. From what I have said it is clear that the present Cabinet has no good reason to attack the late Cabinet in regard to the Americo-Japanese Treaty. As regards the immigration question, the Katsura Cabinet has adopted the policy of its predecessor, so there is nothing to say about it. I intend to treat of the immigration question in a separate chapter.

The American Question

[Count Hayashi appears never to have written the proposed chapter on "The American Immigration Question." His views on the matter may, however, be gathered in part from the following passages in the MSS., presumably contributed to the vernacular press and intended to be embodied in his completed work.—Ed.]

With reference to the anti-Japanese outbreak in California, some Americans were responsible for rumours that a war must occur in the future between the United States and Japan. These Americans support their views by saying that Japan is casting a longing eye on the Philippine Islands and on Hawaii, that the naval supremacy of Japan over America in the Pacific is so great as to make war inevitable, and even that Japan is secretly dispatching disbanded soldiers to Hawaii, with the result, as they allege, that America also is secretly preparing for war.

These rumours do not represent facts. They are only flights of imagination on the part of insignificant local newspapers, whose character is very indifferent. The truly reputable American newspapers repudiate such rumours, showing that there is really no serious difference between the two countries.

Unfortunately, these groundless rumours of war have not only provided a topic of conversation in America but have also given rise to anxiety in Europe.

But if we reflect coolly on the cordial relations which have for so long past existed between America and Japan, we shall find that they remain unchanged. It is true that small differences have arisen, and the Japanese Government has urged on the American Government the advisability of her securing to Japan her proper rights. The anti-Japanese agitation in San Francisco is but a small thing and has nothing to do with the principal question. As regards that affair, everything possible is being done to secure its settlement as speedily as possible. The immigration question is a very simple one to settle. There have been misunderstandings on both sides. The school question was a breach of our treaty rights, but the immigration question was only a matter of faulty police administration in San Francisco, so far as the American authorities are concerned. They have recognized their liabilities toward Japan and have given assurances that similar incidents shall not occur again.

On the Japanese side the situation has been complicated by the action of those Japanese who have emigrated to Hawaii. Under the treaty of 1894 (negotiated when I was Vice-Minister of Foreign Affairs), America could impose restrictions on the immigration of Japanese into America. We strongly objected to this clause, which America tacked on to Article II., but our objections were of no avail. Mr. Griscom, the American Secretary of State, absolutely refused to agree to revise the treaty at all unless the clause was admitted. We were loath to agree, but did so because the revision of the English treaty was problematical on account of the probationary clause, and it was necessary to make a start.

Under the treaty, America could enforce restriction of Japanese immigration, and we can and do enforce similar restrictions.[1]

Before Hawaii became American territory there were many Japanese there. When the island was annexed by the United States the

[1] This did not practically affect America, as the only foreign labourers desirous of entering Japan were Chinese, who were prohibited.—Ed.

Japanese living there transmigrated from Hawaii to California, several thousands each year. The United States authorities have prohibited this transmigration. We believe that our countrymen can so transmigrate, as once they were in Hawaii they were in American territory, where under treaty rights they have freedom of travel.

The Americans refuse to allow this, though by treaty we think that they have no right to do so. On the other hand, if we protest too much, then the United States threaten to close Hawaii to Japanese immigration altogether, which would even be more disadvantageous than the prohibition for Hawaiian Japanese to travel to America.

The American Government has proposed to make a treaty with Japan granting reciprocal rights of immigration. We refused to agree to this and have no intention of giving way. The Cabinet has decided that the only way to settle the immigration question and cognate questions is by the total deletion of the clause at the end of Article II. of the present treaty. In a few years the time will come for the denunciation of that treaty, and a new treaty will be made, which will have no restriction on the freedom of the Japanese to immigrate to America.

It is no good trying to rush matters now, and it is of no value to make a serious question of the damage to Japanese property in San Francisco during the recent riots. When racial prejudices are involved neither side can argue properly, and we must therefore wait till we can discuss the matter in a friendly manner.

In the Hibiya Park riots in 1905 the Japanese destroyed foreign property. But would the Japanese have listened to complaints made at that time? The circumstances are similar.

Racial prejudice, anti-Japanese sentiment, are at the bottom of the San Francisco trouble. All respectable Japanese and Americans are agreed on this matter, but, of course, it is a most difficult thing to sweep away racial prejudice and dislikes.

The matter will be settled satisfactorily. Both Japanese and American statesmen are agreed thereon, and so people can rest quietly. The irresponsible inflammatory language of the newspapers can only complicate the question.

There is no question of Japan being under the dictation of America. We have not agreed to the classification of the Japanese as Mongolians. If the American Government classifies Japanese so, that is its own affair.

As regards the school question we believe this involved a breach of our treaty rights. The matter is, however, very difficult and complicated, and will probably be left for adjustment with the revision of the treaties. Both the Japanese Government and the people remember the long friendship of America for Japan, and are confident that the future will see a satisfactory settlement of it.

We have been greatly helped by the attitude of President Roosevelt. He has done everything possible to obtain a just and wise solution, but naturally he cannot go beyond the powers allowed him by law. He has always set great value on Japanese friendship, and we hope that the evidence he has given of this will strengthen the relations between the two countries. He believes, as we do, that a future war between America and Japan is only journalistic talk, and that a war between the two countries can never take place under any circumstances.

The three questions between Japan and America are the immigration question, the school question, and the problem of China. Not one of these can possibly lead to a war between Japan and the United States.

War can only result from a conflict of interests or of personal feelings or both. Between

America and Japan there is no conflict of either interests or personal feelings which could make war justifiable.

The feelings between the two countries are cordial. Japan regards America as her benefactor, and she is deeply indebted to her for much help and for many improvements. In reality the feelings of Japan for America are as cordial as they were fifty years ago.

There are some people who assert that Japan has ambitions on the Philippines and on Hawaii. Any person possessing common sense can realize what madness it would be for Japan to attempt to deprive so powerful a nation as America of her valuable possessions. There is a tendency, even among persons who ought to know better, to despise America, and to say that she is not a military nation and that her fleet is insignificant. This is a great mistake, for America is a naturally strong country, of immense resources and very rich, and her people are very energetic.

The real problem of the Pacific has nothing to do with Japanese ambitions on the Philippines or any such nonsense. It is the maintenance of the principle of the open door and the territorial integrity of China. On the necessity of maintaining these principles all

Powers are agreed, and the United States is making great efforts to help us to effect them.

Japan fought Russia to maintain the open door in China, and Japan has been the means of ensuring the territorial integrity of China and of opening China to the commerce of the world. She is now beginning to reap the rewards of her labours. The assistance of the United States towards carrying out her objects would be very valuable, and the United States ought to be assured that Japan has no intention of not keeping the pledges that she has given.

The business of diplomacy is not only the conduct of affairs of immediate importance, but should also look to the future. Diplomacy cannot be conducted like a law case and the matter settled in a few days. The opening of China is not a matter of to-day or to-morrow, but a matter of many years.

That is why when we discuss affairs with America we want to discuss all questions together. On the most important question we are agreed. The immigration and school questions which give rise to differences of opinion must be settled by friendly conversations.

To talk of war in such connexion is foolish. There is no particle of cause for a war between

America and Japan, and indeed such rumours
as I have referred to would be unworthy of
attention, except for the wide circulation
which they have attained.

CHAPTER IX

Foreign Policy

PART I

To Bribe or Not to Bribe

In regard to the Russo-Japanese Treaty and Convention, the Franco-Japanese Agreement, and the American-Japanese Agreement, I have already shown in connexion with the last that in its inability to conclude a convention on account of other questions, such as the immigration problem, the Saionji Cabinet committed no fault which would give the Katsura Ministry the right to attack it on the grounds of its foreign policy. In fact, the Katsura Ministry has not been able to make any direct attack on its predecessors on this point.

If there were any points in connexion with foreign affairs on which the Katsura Cabinet might have been able to attack the former

Saionji Ministry, it would have been in reference to its Chinese policy. This attack, however, came not only from members of the Katsura Cabinet but from the Press and from members of the Diet, who raised the Government's Chinese policy in questions in Parliament.

The principal point on which the late Cabinet was attacked was that we had spent in Manchuria several hundred millions of yen and 100,000 lives in order to win our rights and privileges in that country. We ought not, therefore, to be slack in our policy in Manchuria. We ought still to extend further the rights which we have acquired and to strengthen the foundations of our position there, but on no account are we to make China our enemy. The object of Japan ought to be to maintain the peace of the Orient and obtain Chinese goodwill and trust. But as it was alleged, judging from the way in which the Saionji Ministry carried on its business, that Cabinet tried to surrender to China all the privileges which we had gained in Manchuria at the cost of so much of our national energy, whilst simultaneously the anti-Japanese agitation in China and the anti-foreign agitation in China to curtail the rights and privileges which had been ceded to foreigners in that country had gained a great deal of ground and Japan was rapidly losing the confidence of the Chinese. Consequently the enemies of the late Cabinet insisted that we had committed a great diplomatic failure in China and that our diplomatists were quite incapable.

These were the themes of the attacks made against the Saionji Ministry.

When in office we had explained that our attempt to extend our rights and privileges in Manchuria would conflict with the rights of China, and it was natural that if we should try to extend those rights we should lose the confidence of the Chinese, and in any case however far we might want to go in trying to establish our rights, we could not proceed beyond the stipulations in the various treaties, and if we did proceed beyond those stipulations eventually we should have to surrender what we gained.

Again, even though various treaties have gained us special privileges in China, the Chinese will eventually try to limit the sphere of influence as much as possible, whilst we, on our part, must try to reserve as much room for our own expansion in that country as possible. Consequently, it is clear that there is ground for objection from both sides, and

17

it is impossible to avoid ill-feeling and a conflict of interests.

In reply to the explanation of the Cabinet, its opponents said that the fact that we drove the Russians from Manchuria must, in view of our explanation, be considered as an act of magnanimity on the part of Japan for the benefit of the Chinese, and as we had failed to make the Chinese appreciate our service, or to agree to our propositions, we had lost their confidence.

To sum up, the view raised by the opposition, in regard to the Cabinet's foreign policy, was that we ought to get everything for ourselves and at the same time to gain the confidence of the Chinese by making them appreciate our great services in having driven away the Russians.

The mere fact of our replacing the Russians in Manchuria should not be a reason for the Chinese to dislike us. In my opinion such arguments are extremely unreasonable and selfish. That we drove the Russians out of Manchuria was because we wanted to protect our own interests. Our action was necessary for our self-preservation. We were not requested by China to drive Russia out.

Even if we had not taken over the Russian undertakings in Manchuria and were pre-

pared to abandon that country, some other
nation might come in our place, and then we
should be compelled to fight another big
war.

It is, therefore, for our own preservation
that we are holding Manchuria. We have
not acted in the least from humanitarian
considerations. Even the Chinese understand these things. To say that we fought
for China is rather stretching the truth.
There may be some truth in the statement,
but to expect other people to believe it is like
trying "to steal a bell by shutting one's own
ears."

Although we drove the Russians away we
have come in their stead. So, looked at from
the Chinese point of view, we may be likened
to "the wolf that follows the tiger."

From the manner in which the Russians
conducted themselves in Manchuria, it looked
as if they intended to absorb the whole province. We on our side endeavoured to carry
on our work strictly in accordance with the
spirit of the treaty stipulations. Consequently, as a fact there is a great difference
between the positions of the two nations.
From the Chinese standpoint, however, the
difference is only one of degree.

Our critics at home imagine that we may

have yielded too much, and it is, therefore, natural for the Chinese to feel dissatisfied with the arrangement.

The only way to win the confidence of the Chinese is to agree to all the propositions made by their Government.

To insist on one's point of vantage is one thing, to secure the goodwill of the party of the second part is another. It is impossible to carry out both policies. The two have nothing in common. This is true as between individuals and much truer as between nations. We should, however, be careful not to ignore the feelings of others, unless we have good reason to do so.

Now, ever since the occupation of Manchuria by our army there have been frequent instances where we have done things to injure the feelings of the Chinese. To particularize, since the war not only have the roughs and toughs who went to Manchuria from this country maltreated the Chinese there, but even officers of high rank have shown themselves to be men of no moral principle. Not infrequently they have been guilty of acts of gross discourtesy to high Chinese officials.

Such incidents have caused Chinese distrust of us, and are within the scope of a review of our Chinese policy, if it be conducted in accordance with treaty stipulations.

In order to study the feelings of the Chinese towards Japan and Russia with regard to Manchurian affairs, the most important thing to be done is to compare the actions of Japan and Russia towards China. As I have said before in the chapter on the Anglo-Japanese Alliance, when Japan was given the territory of the Yinchow (Liaotung) Peninsula after the war of 27 and 28 Meiji (1894-5), Russia, together with Germany and France, interfered and took the Peninsula away from us and gave it back to China. Besides this she guaranteed the loans of three hundred million taels and thirty million taels, which China had to pay to us, the first sum as indemnity for the war; and the second as the compensation for the return of the Peninsula by us. Consequently, China was able to float this loan in France at the very low rate of 4 per cent. interest.

As a result of this, China was very grateful to Russia, and when she was requested by Russia to fulfil the condition on which the loan was guaranteed, viz., to grant Russia the privilege of constructing the Siberian Railway through the northern part of Manchuria, she consented with a good grace.

Count Muravieff, when he planned the leases of Dairen and Port Arthur and the construction of the railway through Manchuria, had in mind to threaten China by the show of force, but outwardly he let China save her "face."

Again, those Russians who went to Manchuria in the days of Russian supremacy were mostly officials whose salaries were very high and who would spend those salaries lavishly. Again, the work done in the construction of the railway to Port Arthur, in the building of Port Arthur itself, and the construction of Dairen necessitated the expenditure of large sums of money, and the Chinese naturally received considerable benefit from this circulation of money, so the Russians were welcome as the very best customers they could have.

At that time, one of our most prominent statesmen, speaking with Li Hung-Chang, warned him that to allow the Russians this extraordinary freedom in carrying out their plans would ultimately end in the alienation of Chinese sovereignty over Manchuria. To this Li Hung-Chang replied that there was a promise that Manchuria should be returned to China within a certain limit of time, and consequently his countrymen had no need whatever to worry.

As a matter of fact, Li Hung-Chang was by no means well posted in Western affairs, but certainly he was not so ignorant as not to know Russia's real intention. I am certain that he made this answer because he did not know what else to say. He wanted just to save his "face" before his visitor. Why do I think so? Because from the day of that conversation the attitude of the Chinese Government slowly began to change towards Russia and Japan, gradually becoming unfriendly to Russia.

After the Boxer trouble, Russia began to be restless about her eventual success, and openly came out on the side of the occupation of Manchuria, thereby gaining the distinct bad feelings of the Chinese. The Chinese, indeed, at that time began to favour the Japanese, who were raising an army against Russia. But when the Russo-Japanese peace was concluded the Japanese became the successors of the Russians in their various enterprises in Manchuria, and Japan not only got the Yinchow Peninsula again, but also the South Manchurian Railway and the accessories of the peninsula and the railway.

In addition, her general staff established military administrative posts here and there throughout the country and began various undertakings. Now these undertakings were started after the war was over and therefore were, without doubt, outside the scope of military requirements; also, they were made in regions outside the boundary delimited by the Peking Treaty which the Chinese Government had agreed to observe. Besides this, many Japanese entered Manchuria and used to take out all the profits from these undertakings. As a consequence, the attitude of the Chinese towards the Japanese became very unfriendly, and even the Chinese officials began to make protests.

Generally speaking, soldiers who have won battles have done so by making sacrifices, even of what they value most in the world— their own lives. Naturally, they want to gain fame, they want to appropriate, as a result of victory and risk, as many privileges as possible to crown their success in arms. This is only human nature. After the victory of Sadowa by the Prussian army the old Emperor and his Chief of General Staff, von Moltke, and their subordinates, attempted to grab as much profit as possible from Austria. The "blood and iron" Minister, Bismarck, looking far into the future for the days of the unification of the German Empire, was so chagrined at his inability to restrain his soldiers' demands that he walked into his private room and wept, an incident which is recorded in his own memoirs.

It is easy to imagine how boastful and aggressive our soldiers were after the Russo-Japanese War. By what they did there after the war we have lost not only the goodwill of the Chinese, but have also won the adverse criticism of Europeans and Americans.

It cannot be denied that such conduct disturbs the smooth working of diplomacy. It is true that M. Kato (later Baron), the then Foreign Minister, resigned his position, and, as it was stated, did this on account of his opposition to the nationalization of the railways, but his resignation was also due to the fact that he was sandwiched in between the two opposing forces at work at home and abroad in regard to Manchurian affairs.

Also the visit which Marquis Saionji, when Premier, secretly made to Manchuria, was because he wanted to investigate the condition of affairs personally. Under these circumstances, no one who was placed in the public position of Minister of Foreign Affairs could have succeeded in further extending our privileges and at the same time preventing our losing the goodwill of the Chinese.

It was on May 19, 1906 (39 Meiji), that I

was appointed Minister of Foreign Affairs
after my return from England, and on May
22d a conference of the Genro was held at
which were present Princes Ito, Yamagata,
Oyama, and Marquis Matsukata and Marquis
Inouye, all the members of the Cabinet, Prince
Katsura, Admiral Yamamoto, and the Chief
of the General Staff, the late General Kodama.

After a lengthy deliberation it was decided
to abolish the military administrative staff
as soon as possible and to evacuate the
regions outside the territory delimited by
the Treaty of Peking; and it was also decided
that this evacuation should take place even
before the date fixed in the treaty, and those
regions should be returned as soon as possible
to the Chinese authorities. It is, however,
only human nature to hanker after undertakings which have once been begun. Then
it must be remembered that the undertakings in Manchuria had been carried on
for nearly a year, and the people of the regions
which had been under our administration
during this time had in due course entered
into various complicated relationships with
our officials.

It was, therefore, a most difficult thing to
carry out the decisions of this Genro council.
Negotiation after negotiation was conducted

and slowly the programme was carried out. These negotiations included matters which not only concerned China, but such other matters as the officials in Saghalien, the Red Cross Hospital in Port Arthur, the temples and burial grounds and other things concerning Russia, which took a long time to discuss.

As regards our attitude towards China, the negotiations were very difficult owing to the many unreasonable things that our soldiers had done after their victory. During the administration of the Saionji Cabinet most of the points arising from the war and the post-bellum events in Manchuria were disposed of. The Foreign Office had taken as reasonable an attitude towards China as political conditions at home would permit them to do, and there remain to-day but very few points which have not been finally cleared up.

To be sure, Chinese diplomacy is often treacherous, so we were prepared to beat the Chinese at their own game. We could not say on every occasion, "Yes, yes, we agree," to whatever the Chinese asked. Besides, in those days there arose, from other circumstances, an anti-foreign agitation in China, having for its object the curtailment of the concessions granted to foreigners, and along with this general anti-foreign agitation came a specific anti-Japanese agitation, which assumed serious features. As a consequence, our negotiations became doubly difficult.

It was practically impossible to win the goodwill of the Chinese unless we were willing to agree to every proposition made by them. Of course, if you are prepared to agree to everything that the other side asks, negotiation is the simplest matter in the world. I think that the demands of our countrymen that we should always gain the goodwill of the Chinese arose from the fact that we were not willing to deceive the Chinese, and the Opposition in Japan blamed the Government for that.

As China is the fountain source of one of the greatest civilizations in the world, one must recognize that civilized institutions and customs are already there. On the other hand, the Japanese have imported the civilization of the West only during recent years and have imitated it, and they may think when they go to China and associate with the Chinese that they are really in no way inferior to the latter.

But if the Japanese will only strip off their

gold braid they will find that they have
left only that which they have imported
originally from China, and consequently it is
clear that they are behind the Chinese in
every point of civilization. Certainly, we
have our peculiar ideas of national solidarity
and the spirit of Bushido which has been
with us ever since the prehistoric period.

In these respects we do not stand behind
any other nation in the world, but what I
mean is that in the degree of social civilization
we must admit, however reluctantly, that
China is far richer than Japan. If we see
the Chinese in foreign countries we find them
endeavouring to adjust themselves to the
circumstances surrounding them, and, therefore, they are very cautious of what they
say and do. So aside from the fact that they
dress differently there is nothing in them to
attract our attention.

But if we go to Peking and associate with
the high officials of that country, we find
that we have entered a world entirely different from ours in Japan. The houses, the
dresses, the social manners, even the methods
of entering and leaving, are all established
with the strictest regularity. On those
Westerners who have grown up under purely
Occidental civilization, these things may not

make any very striking impression, but to the Japanese who have braided Western civilization over their Chinese civilization, they cause some peculiarly awesome feelings.

Certainly it may be a little different as regards the young men who have been brought up in the new atmosphere of the Meiji era, but even they may not be able to get away entirely from the impressions that I have suggested. Besides, those Chinese who are in the upper strata of society, though differently educated from us, are all very well educated. They are not bumptious or conceited as the Japanese are, but they are very large-minded, learned and leisurely, and skilful in the use of diplomatic language. Besides, their standard of living is very much higher than that of the Japanese, and consequently, if we enter Chinese society, while we may lose sight of the Western civilization, we will gradually become assimilated into the Chinese style and unconsciously become "Chinasized" and in the end will sympathize with things Chinese.

Thus it is that we have with us people who have been feasted by the Chinese and told in the characteristic language of Chinese diplomacy that China and Japan are like "the wagon and its wheels," or "a man's

teeth and his lips," that "our country (China)
is far behind in the ways of Western civilization and must look up to Japan for guidance
and bringing up," and other such good things,
and they (the Japanese) straightway become
elated and at once decide that it is a mistake
to say that it is impossible to come to friendly
terms with the Chinese. As a result they
make up their minds that our diplomatic
methods are altogether wrong, and that the
Chinese are not at all unreasonable nor are
they obstinate, that the anti-foreign agita-
tions in that country are due to the unreason-
ableness of the foreigners, for which the
Chinese are not to blame, that we should
yield what we should yield and leave unimportant things and hold on to the main
things we want, since the development and
guidance of China is the mission of Japan.
Optimists come back to Japan and bluster
these generalities from one end of the country
to the other.   They think they know everything there is to be known about China and
the Chinese. It is through the efforts of
such men that we have eventually had proposals even to bamboozle the Chinese.

Such blundering critics can give no good
advice to the country or to those who are in
office, especially at a time when diplomatic

negotiations are being engaged in. If we were to follow their advice and yield anything to obtain the goodwill of the Chinese, then we should have to be prepared to yield everything. What we can afford to yield is just what China does not want, and what they want is just what we must have. These people have been misled by the Chinese expressions and by such words as "we want your guidance," "we want your help," etc., etc., which are used by the Chinese mostly as a matter of deference.

On their part they use them in a spirit of humility, but for us in Japan to publish them broadcast in the newspapers, and to quote them in our addresses is really a great insult to our neighbours and does serious harm to our diplomatic work. These points ought to be brought home to the Japanese, if they would but think a little. Up to only fourteen or fifteen years ago, China was considered by the Chinese themselves as being far superior to Japan. Even when China was defeated in the war with Japan and temporarily cast down a little, they had not really at heart come to admit their defeat. If we could place ourselves in the Chinese position we could understand this and appreciate it.

It is not true when they say, "We want to be guided and educated by the Japanese," and again it would be useless for us to attempt the policy of "bamboozle," which can only be done in the case of uncivilized barbarians. To adopt such a policy towards China would be the height of insult to the intelligence of a nation which stands on equal terms with us. If the Chinese get the notion into their head that they have been insulted by such a policy, it would do a lot of harm to our diplomatic work.

That the Chinese employ the Japanese as teachers is not because they want the Japanese, or that they want to be educated and guided by the Japanese. The real reason is that they employ the Japanese because the latter can be secured for small salaries, and although the Japanese talk big things, as a matter of fact they are generally much more easily managed than the Occidentals. Whether the number of Japanese teachers employed throughout China be large or small, it does not make very much difference in raising Japanese prestige. The Chinese are to blame for trying to employ teachers at small salaries. Many of these teachers go about to ingratiate themselves with petty officials in order to win the latter's favour;

18

mostly that they may report bad things about other teachers in order to raise themselves in the eyes of the Chinese, and this sort of ugly behaviour has been indulged in very often by the Japanese teachers in China.

I mention these things (with regard to the Japanese teachers in China) because they hurt the dignity of the nation, and because in the 24th session of the Diet there were some members who attacked the Saionji Ministry for having failed in diplomacy because Japanese teachers were discharged from China. Even some officials of the Government lent their ears to these complaints. What a blunder!

There are also those who think that they know the short cut to success in this world, and advocate the employment of bribery and corruption to win over the high officials of the Chinese Government, and by the aid of these means to accomplish their diplomatic ends. There are those who say that in Chinese official circles bribery was resorted to for the recognition of Russia in Manchuria.

Of course, such arguments are not used publicly, but I judge that the very spirit of the men who advocate trying such methods on the high officials of the Government of our neighbour is a source of our failure.

Besides this, I think they are misinformed as to the practice of bribery in Chinese official circles. In the first place, when the Chin dynasty unified and established the Government, the officials of that Government, taking a warning from the results of the extravagance of the officials of the Ming dynasty, solemnly resolved not to follow in the footsteps of their predecessors.

The Ministers of State, in order to give an example to their descendants, instructed the artists of those days to draw pictures of the Manchus on scrolls. I saw some of these scrolls whilst I was in Peking, and I judged that the standard of living as represented by the pictures was about the same as that of the Mongols of to-day.

I noticed when I went to Peking twelve or thirteen years ago that those public buildings, roads, and sewers of the city which were constructed on a grand scale and were splendid in appearance, have now been destroyed or left in disgraceful condition without any attempt to repair them. It was explained to me that this has been because the later-day Manchus had misunderstood the meaning of the warnings against extravagance and of the admonitions to be economical. Such (economy and frugality) was the policy of the Manchus in the beginning of their rule. So the salary of the officials was very small. This policy is maintained even to-day. To illustrate by one or two examples. The annual income of an official of the Order of the First Degree of the first and second ranks, as the Imperial Tutor, the Emperor's chief attendant, the professors of the Imperial University, the tutor of the Crown Prince and the attendants of the Crown Prince, and the Ministers of State, amounts to only 545 taels, 60 cheng. At the exchange of one tael to Yen 1.50, this sum translated into Japanese currency amounts to Yen 818.40 (=£81 10s.).

The Viceroys of provinces, who are of the Order of the Second Degree of the first rank, and the military governors who are of the Second Degree of the second rank, receive yearly 498 taels, 45 cheng, which translated into terms of Yen, is Y. 747.60 (=£74 7s. 6d.). It is true the Viceroys and military governors receive certain extra pay (in the form of "encouragement for frugality"), but the regular and the extra pay together are not enough to maintain their official dignity.

In the earlier days of the Manchu rule the officials met the people with the pride of conquerors and they could manage to live somehow.

It may have been that such a policy was originally a better one to spur men to greater efforts. When the Romans governed a foreign country they took a pride in their poverty, but when they began to enjoy the fruits of their military success, they became extravagant. It was just the same with the Manchus. When the Manchus began to receive the influence of the Chinese civilization and to associate with the Chinese of the richer classes, they began to feel the pinch of their insufficient salaries and to see that they could not therewith maintain their dignity.

When I was in Peking, Li Hung-Chang was the great doctor of learning, and Minister of State for Foreign Affairs. He was living in a Buddhist temple called "Shien Liang Shii." His salary was that of an official of the First Degree of the first rank, but as Minister of State for Foreign Affairs he received an extra sum of 1000 taels, for, as it was officially termed, "encouragement of frugality." If one visited the "Shien Liang Shii" temple one would find that some of the cottages of the monks had been rented and offices installed there, whilst ten of Li's servants or relatives would also live in such little houses. There were also to be found several tens of riding horses and asses in company with a few officers, who officially received Yen 500 (£50) or more, and who were his supporters. These men, however, were all paid by Li Hung-Chang.

When I went to call on him there I was shown into a sort of rest room, which was not very spacious, the bed being rather coarse and cheap, similar to those used in soldiers' barracks. The floors were bare, there being no rugs, and the chairs were of hard wood in plain Western style.

Li Hung-Chang, when I entered, was sitting on a rubber air cushion. He arose and offered me the cushion, but I said, "I am a young man and do not need it! You are an old man, so do not mind me, continue to sit on it as you were doing when I entered." "I have been ill, with piles," he said, "and cannot very well sit, so please excuse me," and resumed the cushion. On the floor to his right were scattered sundry books on international law by Chi, books on astrological studies and other things. On the desk were to be seen brushes, ink blocks, papers, envelopes, etc. Such was the simple furnishing of his work room.

His life was a very simple one, but the amount of money which he used to spend every month in keeping up the dignity of his position easily reached several thousand taels. As for the high officials whose manner of life was very extravagant and luxurious and who loved scrolls of writing and pictures and articles of antiquity, it is quite impossible to estimate how much was spent by them.

Mr. Shii was the teacher of calligraphy to the Emperor Kwang Hsu and used to live in the Chio Ming Chang Palace where the Japanese Legation was formerly situated. He used to keep on his premises about 300 servants, and the director of the Hanlin, whom I used to know, received about Yen 40 per month as salary, but every month he spent from Yen 500 to 600 for bare living expenses.

Such a state of affairs was due to the fact that the officials were compelled to incur high expenses owing to the general high standard of living, but as their salaries, which were fixed by the official system, created centuries ago and long continued without any change, cannot be altered, the officials are compelled to get extra revenues from somewhere else.

The result was that the Peking officials would take tribute money from the Provincial officials and the Provincial officials would take tribute money from the people.

In the west, too, in olden times, there were

systems by which the collection of Provincial taxes was farmed out on a commission basis. Those who undertook the work would pay to the Government a certain fixed sum, and they could exact as much as they could get for themselves. And then again, officials would perform various offices for different people in connection with other official duties, and then take commission from these people for the services rendered. These systems eventually came to be recognized as a part of the system of salaries. Such a system is, indeed, a very bad one, but it cannot necessarily be called one of bribery.

It is true that the Chin Government is an antiquated and despotic Government. It has many deep-rooted iniquities, and it may be true that bribery flourished under it, but as regards the system of salaries which I have tried to describe above, it cannot be said that bribery is practised openly in China.

We often hear people say that in order to meet an official in China one has to attach a five-dollar note to one's visiting card; otherwise the servants of the house would not usher a visitor in.

When I was in Peking I heard that in order to meet a Prince of the blood or a high official, a Chinese would have to attach a fifty-dollar note to his visiting card, but even these cases cannot be called bribes. It would be more correct to call them a bad system of commissions which was general throughout the country.

In olden times the Chinese used to say of the Japanese that "the Japanese can afford to be unstained because their salaries are high." I think that unless we begin to pay some serious attention to our official system of salaries, some very bad customs may develop in the future.

But it would be a disgraceful thing if we attempted to attain our diplomatic ends by the use of money in dealing with high officials merely because there is a system of open bribery or commission such as I have just explained. Supposing, for argument's sake, that we decided to bribe them, the amounts which would be required to move the high officials of the Chin dynasty would be far greater than the sums paid as bribes by the Japan Sugar Refinery Company which paid yen 200 to yen 300 and yen 20,000.

Just think of it! The price of the honour of our noted men is indeed very cheap. But in China such men would not sell themselves so cheaply. Of course, this is only a suppositious case to make the matter more easily understood.

Let us suppose again that Russia has really used bribes to buy up the high officials of China. After the Chino-Japanese War, when the Triple Alliance interfered and helped to have the Liaotung Peninsula returned to China, the amount of bonds issued in Paris was 330,000,000 taels, including the amounts which had to be paid as war indemnity and the purchase price for the return of the Liaotung Peninsula. The bonds were issued bearing interest at 4 per cent. They were guaranteed by the Russian Government, and were sold at 98 francs per 100 francs face value, as far as I remember. What was the net amount received by the Chinese Government I do not know, as this was kept secret, but at the very highest it could not have been more than 90. There was, therefore, a difference of 8 francs, or 8 per cent. The whole issue was a little over yen 300,000,000.

Eight per cent. on that would be 28,800,000 yen, and on that amount interest assessed, and the expenses for printing the bonds, for taxes and miscellaneous expenses, would not be very much in comparison. Supposing it were yen 2,000,000, there would still be left yen 26,800,000 to be accounted for. This last figure represents what went to the banks and the financiers who were interested in making the issue. Supposing the amount were shared with the Chinese, the latter would have got yen 13,400,000, or, if they only got 10 per cent. on the difference between the net and the gross price, they would have got yen 2,680,000. A bribe of such a large amount might indeed be effective in bringing about the signature of a contract for the construction of railroads in Manchuria.

If Russia had really resorted to such methods of bribery, it follows then since she has established the Chinese-Eastern Bank in Peking and conducted business in the characteristic way of Russia, she must have continued ever since that policy of bribery in accordance with the precedent of the Paris bond issue.

Now, granting that the suggestions of those who advise our Government to bribe the Chinese officials were to be taken, and the incident mentioned with regard to Russia were true, could Japan in her present position employ any such large bribes? Even if Russia had employed this method of bribery, if we consider what is the attitude of the Chinese towards Russia, it cannot be said that the Chinese were well disposed towards Russia. They were only compelled by the force of circumstances to yield to the Russian proposals, and once they found that they could not endure it any longer they looked around for some other nations to come to their aid.

Regarding the negotiations about the Russian evacuation of South Manchuria, my colleague at St. Petersburg, Yang Ji, was grief-stricken and died, I think, on that account. To buy the high officials of a neighbouring country with bribes had been practised during the days of the Bourbons in France, as history relates, but in these days when budgets are decided in Parliament such methods can never be practised.

As regards our own country, in the first place we have no resources for such a fund, and even if we had such a fund available it would consist of only a few hundred thousand yen, which might be used as a special fund for the high purposes of State, but such an insignificant sum would be quite insufficient for any great purpose. The difficult point in dealing with the Chin Government is somewhere else, and has no relation whatever to bribery or Machiavellism or firm attitude, bamboozling, or any other such nonsense.

CHAPTER X

Foreign Policy *(Continued)*

PART II

FRIEND "PIDGIN"

CHINA for ages past has been boasting to the surrounding foreign countries about her being the celestial land. She has had the habit of making much of herself in a proud and haughty manner, so even when she was attacked by a foreign Power and was unable to resist the aggressions she still kept proud and haughty.

When the Ching and Han dynasties entered China from foreign countries, these, in their turn, became proud and haughty. In the case of the Chin dynasty it was the same. When a Government is powerful the pride of the officials of that Government may be excused by other persons on account of the Government's power, but as soon as that

Government loses its power other parties will not remain submissive. In China civil society is held in much higher esteem than military society.

As soon as temporary warfares are put an end to, she will not be able to boast to foreign countries about herself. But the Government would like to hide that fact from its nationals, so the officials are always trying to save the face of the nation by any means. This "saving of face" is the first consideration of Chinese officials in any diplomatic dealings in which they may be engaged.

Supposing an incident happens. If the Chinese Government should yield only 20 per cent. of what is demanded, the remainder could be left undisturbed, yet as the officials are anxious to save the national face they do not like to yield, and eventually China loses the whole 100 per cent.

From the point of view of the Chinese they are not by any means, so to say, the party of the first part, to seek intercourse with foreign countries. They would much rather not have the foreigners within their confines. But foreigners come to China on their own account and stir up various difficulties, so it is the foreigners and not the

Chinese that make the various requests. Consequently there is a call for an agitation for the expulsion of foreigners or for closing up the Treaty Ports. Yet they are not able to meet the foreigners with the point of the bayonet, and China must therefore drag along indefinitely because they do not know what else they can do.

That is the essence of Chinese foreign policy, and if any incident brings matters to a critical condition then she would employ Machiavellism and play one Power off against another, herself remaining in between and gathering the profits for herself. That is to say, she uses the method of playing two tigers off against each other. Well, if even one tiger dies and the other is wounded there is not enough strength left in China to drive off the wounded tiger. So, even if she employs the plan of playing two nations off against each other, in the end she will be pressed to the wall by one or the other of the two countries engaged. Even if there should be intelligent Ministers in the Government who could see this point clearly, and who tried to yield what is inevitable and settle matters quickly, the other class who always insist upon saving the face of the country would come out with the most bitter criticism of the Ministers, who would soon be unable to hold their positions, and indeed would find it impossible to maintain their heads on their bodies.

Now what is the "face" which they want to save? It is really that they want to carry through their proud and haughty manner as of old; they are not satisfied with standing on equal terms with foreign countries. Such a state of affairs can be found (to some extent) in almost every country. Those who are in diplomatic positions of trust will often find themselves sandwiched between the people at home and foreign countries, but in China it is carried to the extreme. That is the main difficulty which foreign diplomatists have in dealing with China.

The officials of the Chinese Government, even if they should be men of intelligence, would therefore keep postponing matters and postponing them until they got pressed to the wall and then they would refer it to the high council of the Government, and only then comply with the demands made upon them, and because there is no other alternative. No one shoulders any responsibility and finally the matters get settled in this way. If they settle matters too soon they might lose the national "face," and then if they lost

the national "face," foreign nations would
scorn them, thereby leaving a bad example
to posterity.

When I was dealing with China I well
knew this inevitable circumstance, but, nevertheless, I continued my negotiations persistently. The Ministers of the Foreign
Office at Peking are individually men of
intelligence, and all understand what is good
and what is bad for the country. During
the negotiations I had with China I found
that the men who had the power of quick
decision were Li Hung-Chang and Shu Yun
Yi. When I say they had the power of quick
decision it must be understood that it was
comparative in accordance with the importance of the matter under discussion, and
when it came to really big matters it cannot be
said that even these officials were capable of
quick decisions. It was all a matter of degree.

The man whom I admired a great deal
for having the power of very clear judgment
was Prince Kun of earlier times. He might,
indeed, be called a man of genius. He was
a man whose position was very firmly established and what he did could not ever have
been done by any other official, high or low
in the Government.

Whilst circumstances in the official world

19

in Peking are such as I have described, foreign Powers are unable to do anything except take up the position of defendant, because the position of plaintiff would be a losing one. The foreign Powers must decide to be prepared to stay always in a defensive position, so that whichever way affairs may be settled they should not lose, and they must be prepared to wait as long as China wants to wait, for hurry with China certainly results in loss.

For the Press abroad, without considering these things at all, to say that matters between China and foreign countries must be solved immediately, or it would be a loss for the foreign country, shows no understanding of Chinese diplomacy. It would mean, indeed, that such advice was tendered only as an attack on the Government and its acceptance would be a serious thing. Newspaper attacks on diplomatists, who are conducting negotiations with China, only result in tying the hands of the officials. To be sure the negotiations might unduly drag on, which could result in a conflict of feelings, which would be far more endurable than injured feelings due to the publication of self-satisfied accounts of how China wants us to guide them and educate them, or other such useless nonsense.

Such diplomatic issues as exist to-day between Japan and China must arise from time to time. We have to be prepared for them. There is no reason to worry that such incidents might cause trouble in the relationship between the two countries. Even if the trouble came it would not be our fault alone. China would also have to share the responsibility. If we are constantly accused of being all wrong and of hurting the feelings of China, then the only thing the Ministry can do to relieve the tension would be to yield every point that the Chinese claim.

It is no use for the newspapers or the opposition to attack the late Saionji Ministry on account of its Chinese policy and to demand a reform of Japanese diplomatic methods, as it did in August and September last (1907), to advocate the winning of Chinese friendship by a sympathetic policy. One result of this is, as has been frequently testified, that the Chinese in Peking all believed that the Katsura Ministry when it came into power would accept without delay all the demands made by China. That is the evidence of men who live in Peking.

It does not matter which Ministry is in power diplomatic matters cannot be accomplished in a hurry. The Chinese found that

292 Secret Memoirs of Count Hayashi

the attacks on the Saionji foreign policy by the Opposition did not mean that the Japanese disapproved of that policy; they found that Japan had deceived them, or so it appeared to them. She was greatly disappointed and the negotiations have continued to drag on.

In general it is a very great mistake to attack any Government on its foreign policy unless there is a very definite point at issue. For it simply means that the foreign policy of the Government is being used as a plank of the platform of the party for party reasons and in party quarrels.

In dealing with China we want to take plenty of time to regard all the provincial and local problems of that country, to insist upon our claims and to explain patiently and steadily the reasons for the position we take up. We should be ready to reciprocate in yielding and then wait until the convention is finally signed. We ought not to boast and brag to the Chinese, for thereby we only hurt their feelings. To the Ministers of State and gentlemen of China we should be polite in our manner and should try to cultivate a warm friendship. There is no other way to success.

We are told, perhaps, that China has now turned her attention towards Russia, or, perhaps, towards Germany. These things ought not to trouble us. It is a waste of time to trouble ourselves about them. It is only China's old game of playing one tiger against another.

As I have said before, the only thing to do is to be calm, not to get jealous, and to wait. Whichever Ministry is in power, Saionji or Katsura, it ought to make no difference to our foreign policy. It is not plausible to attack the foreign policy of a Ministry on mere hearsay information.

My dissertation on the Chinese policy has become rather long.

I shall end it with a brief outline of the *Tatsu Maru* incident. As I have often had to speak on this matter, I do not mean to go into details.

On board the *Tatsu Maru* was cargo shipped by Chinese and foreigners, and including some cases shipped by Japanese. In these latter cases were rifles, the consignee of which resided in Amoy. All bills of lading and other documents were in perfect condition. When this vessel was lying at anchor in the neighbourhood of Amoy waiting for the tide, Chinese military officers came up in a steam launch and boarded the *Tatsu Maru*. They pulled down the Japanese flag and seized the vessel, convoying it to Canton. The reason given was that the *Tatsu Maru* had arms aboard which were intended to be used by rebels inland.

But to place an embargo on contraband of war is permitted only during the time of war when either belligerent or neutral vessels can be seized. No nation has any right to seize contraband merely because there is a rebellion within its territories. She has certainly no right to capture the vessel of a foreign country and seize its cargo, even if the cargo does consist of arms. It may be imagined that China could have seized the arms when they were landed from the Japanese vessel and could have used them itself to assist in putting down the rebellion.

The action of the Chinese officers was just that of pirates.

The Saionji Cabinet recognized that there was a rebellion in the interior of China and knew well the conditions in the interior. They sympathized with the officials of the province affected; they were willing for the provincial officials to buy the arms if they were not willing to let them go to the rebels, and they were willing to assist in negotiating with the sellers; but also they insisted that China should indemnify the owners of the ship and apologize for the insult done to the Japanese flag, according to established custom.

On the other hand, the Japanese Government, which had issued regulations with regard to the shipment of arms to China, agreed to prohibit the shipments to Amoy. The incident was settled on this basis. If that arrangement had not been considered satisfactory we should have had no alternative but to surrender the shipment of arms to China as she had captured them, and leave the insult to the flag unsatisfied. In addition, the damage done to the owner of the ship would not have been indemnified, whilst the Japanese Government would have had to indemnify other foreigners for damage done to their cargoes.

There seems to me only these two alternatives. If we had adopted the latter, the Chinese, of course, would have been glad, but the Japanese certainly would not have been satisfied. That the Saionji Cabinet, taking all the circumstances into consideration, took mild steps in this affair, seems to me very proper. I believe it was a fair and impartial thing to do, and it was most unreasonable of the Kwantung officials to declare a boycott against Japanese goods. But it is actions such as these which cause China to be scorned by foreign nations.

CHAPTER XI

The Powers and China

[A considerable portion of the following chapter was published by Count Hayashi in the *Chuo-Koron* in November, 1908.—ED.]

BEFORE the Chino-Japanese War, China was regarded as the sleeping lion of Asia, but the war showed that far from being a lion China was only a sleeping badger. It was as a consequence of the Chino-Japanese War that the period of the territorial partition of China took place.

Germany acquired the lease of the Kiao-chow territory in Shantung, Russia seized Port Arthur and Kwantung, whilst France obtained the rectification of her frontier in the region of Annam.

The outstanding feature of Far Eastern politics at that time was the combined pressure on China of the Triple Alliance of Russia, Germany, and France. The United States,

England, and Japan were not parties to that combination, and indeed looked on it with considerable misgiving and suspicion. As, however, these three countries were not then in a position to take any decisive action in the matter, the situation remained without amelioration until the Boxer Rebellion of 1900.

Who actually instigated that rebellion is unknown, but there is no doubt that Russia must be held principally responsible by the Powers, if for no other reason than that she did not warn them, when she well knew that the rising was imminent.

More important, however, than the ques-. tion of who instigated the rebellion is the question of what induced China to resort to such violent measures in order to drive the Powers out of China.

The explanation is that China realized that the Powers were divided amongst themselves, and that the two groups were in constant antagonism. So it may be said that the Boxer Rebellion, was caused by the friction between the two groups of Powers and the constant clashing of their interests. This gave China the opportunity of setting up a counter-balance to the ambitions of the Powers, and of asserting for herself a dominating position.

China, however, went too far. The rebellion became so serious that all the Powers were forced to combine and to work harmoniously together. In the face of a union of all the Powers, China trembled and abjectly sued for peace.

The result was that an enormous indemnity was paid, strong Legation guards were posted in Peking, and a fort was erected in the compound of the German Legation, which commanded the Imperial Palace. That was the work of the Powers working together in unison. It was a lesson from which the Powers could learn that if they all acted together they could obtain whatever advantages they wanted from China. But if they worked independently they were certain to be completely baffled.

Railways, mining concessions, teaching appointments and privileges, the import and export of merchandise, are all lucrative enterprises, which the Powers could control if they did not always fight and wrangle over their acquisition. As soon as the Powers begin to dispute amongst themselves, China uses her time-honoured policy of harnessing the opposing forces and driving them at her own sweet will.

Some Japanese say that English influence

in China is declining. I would not go so far
as that, but certainly I would agree that
English influence is not gaining ground in
China. It must be said that even European
influence generally is not so strong in China
as it was. But if European influence is losing its position in China it is because the
European Powers are always competing
amongst themselves, and stultifying their
own endeavours.

Instead of each nation looking after its own
business, the European nations are always
engaged in looking after their neighbours'
business and in trying to depreciate their
neighbours' business and interests.

For example, Japan undertook certain enterprises in Manchuria, which she had legally
acquired and which had been recognized by
China as being hers. But certain English
firms and individuals were also seeking to
start commercial undertakings in that country, which conflicted with Japan's lawful
undertakings. These people, though themselves engaged in a wrongful undertaking,
endeavoured to make out that Japan was in
the wrong and actually appealed to China on
the point. What is the result? China sees
that in spite of the treaty of alliance between
Japan and England, the interests of those

two countries can be opposed to each other. Consequently her ambitions to set off England against Japan are encouraged. This is only one instance out of many which I could relate.[1]

Some diplomats are so zealous for the advancement of the interests of their own country that they forget everything else. Such zeal is certainly excellent and praiseworthy, but when such diplomats go so far as to disparage openly the rights of other Governments to the Chinese Government, then the latter is easily able to recognize that the interests of the different Powers are in opposition, and intrigues to set the one against the other. In such cases it is very easy work for China to outwit the Powers.

When I was Minister at Peking I proposed to China to introduce a law for the registration of trademarks. The British Minister seconded my proposal. The German Minister, however, for some unknown reason, refused to agree to the proposal and so nothing was done in the matter. Nowadays there is a great number of fraudulent trademarks on the Chinese markets, and the Japanese are

[1] Count Hayashi obviously refers to the Fa-ku-men Railway affair. It was the first important incident which went to assure the world that Japanese pledges to maintain the open door were only scraps of paper, and that the Anglo-Japanese Alliance's reiteration of the same was merely a polite formula.—ED.

accused of being the counterfeiters of them. Such an allegation impairs the honour of Japan.

Incidents such as these reveal the discords between the Powers, and the Chinese are not so slow-witted as not to take advantage of them.

A similar situation is seen to-day in regard to the outcry against Japanese trade which is being made in America. The Manchurian markets came under the control of Japan because her methods of trading are very good. But the Americans are jealous of our success and complain that Japan is monopolizing the trade of Manchuria. Extremists in the United States even go so far as to threaten us, and urge that an alliance be made between the United States and China.

Such dissensions are fatal to the true interests of the Powers, for they enable China to attack them in vital parts.

Events in history have repeatedly proved that if only the Powers combine against China, they can dictate any terms to her. But if they act inharmoniously and independently then they will be sadly outwitted by that country. Repeated experiences of such nature ought to have taught the Powers bitter lessons.

The attitude of the Powers towards China has of recent years undergone considerable change. This has put their acting in unison quite within the limits of possibility. Nowadays political considerations are of minor importance, as compared with economic considerations.

Russia, in order to satisfy the schemes of a court clique, converted the barren wastes of Siberia into a colony, and acquired an ice-free port on the Pacific. No other Power in the world would attempt such a useless task.

It is true that England holds Wei-hai-Wei, and Germany has acquired a lease of Kiao-chow. But both places are of very minor importance commercially and both Powers would be glad to get rid of them, if they could do so without loss of prestige. The same is true with regard to the American possession of the Philippine Islands, and as a matter of fact the feeling in America against keeping the islands is strong and grows stronger every year.

The policy of the Powers in China is the expansion of the commercial spheres. There is no longer any desire to obtain control of parts of China, for China is a very difficult country to manage and the population is very large.

No Power in these days wants to partition China, and Japan wants it least of all. Partition would mean a general conflagration. Of course China might force a partition, but it is not likely, and the Powers would be very reluctant to accept the suggestion.

China is a country of obscurity. It is impossible to know what China really wants, for she seems to think it a disgrace to dissolve the mystery with which she surrounds herself even to her best friends. It is not, therefore, surprising that the outside world is not easily able to get the exact truth with regard to occurrences in that country.

The foreign representatives in Peking try assiduously to learn the state of affairs, but with but poor success. The late rebellion (Anhui) may produce grave results, or it may be really only a flash in the pan. Any deductions with regard to China are always rash, and it is quite premature to say that the rising will produce a great, far-reaching disturbance in the Extreme East.

The attitude of the Powers towards China must be considered in relation to the internal conditions of the country.

The two most successful revolutions in the history of the world have been those of Peter the Great in Russia and of the Meiji Restora-

tion in Japan. The rising in Anhui has no
sort of resemblance to either of them.

But there is another point of great potential
importance. The late Emperor of China
gave an Imperial Rescript to his people, pro-
mising the inauguration of representative
government in nine years. As he is dead
it is doubtful whether that promise will be
realized as it had been intended.

In despotic countries, like China or Russia,
the succession of a wise sovereign to the throne
imports great deeds both at home and abroad.
But when the Government rests in the hands
of a sovereign of only ordinary intelligence,
it but affords opportunity for the intrigues
of men who are anxious to increase their
political power or even for men who have no
political power to obtain some.

It is true that China annually sends many
young men abroad to study, and later after
their return they receive appointments in the
Government service. But these appointments are generally only technical, and the
real administration remains in the hands of
men who are generally incapable, for they
have only old-fashioned ideas of government. So long as such men keep the reins of
government reform in the administration is
impossible.

The late Empress Dowager and the late
Emperor represent two opposing political
factions. These have now been both removed, and China may, perhaps, no longer
be a scene of trouble, but her future may indeed reveal many rapid changes, especially
in the administrative spheres.

But even if the representative government
promised by the late Emperor never material-
izes, it has already commenced to evolve a
very important change, which must affect
the situation in regard to the Powers. In
all grades of Chinese society preparations
have been made for the inauguration of representative government. Newspapers are now
being published everywhere, and political
parties are being formed in all the provinces.

What better and more popular motto
could all these parties choose than restoration
to China of the rights acquired by the foreigners? No more inspiring text could be
imagined.

Of course the Chinese authorities may not
approve of such a war-cry for the young
politicians. On the other hand, it might
suit them very well to encourage it and so to
distract attention from the mismanagement
and maladministration of the country and
to focus the public mind on foreign affairs.

20

An anti-foreign agitation, which is the true name of the rights recovery movement, is always popular in China. Such an agitation finds a great field and would extend as China grew to realize her riches and resources. The heaviest sufferers would be the Powers.

Past experience in China only serves to strengthen my apprehensions. Japan defeated China severely in the Chino-Japanese War, but the punishment which China then received was not sufficiently severe to teach her how weak she really is. Nor was it sufficient to prevent her starting the Boxer Rebellion against foreigners. To crush that rebellion the Powers combined and the Imperial House was humbled to the dust. But even then the lesson was not sufficiently severe for China. This is seen by the objections which she now raises to the Russian administration in Harbin, to the Japanese administration and rights in Manchuria, to German enterprise at Kiaochow, and by the boycott of American and Japanese goods in the south of China.

The day will come when China will rise against England. As that Power has the greatest interests in China it stands to reason that she will suffer the heaviest losses of any of the Powers.

It is high time for the Powers to take to heart the lessons of their bitter experiences.

Some Japanese are so foolish as even to advise the authorities to be "mild" in their treatment of China, and to befriend and conciliate that country.   Such advice is supreme folly.   China is not a savage tribe in the South Sea Islands, but a great Empire, diplomatically even superior to the great Empires of Europe.

It is impossible to trick China into doing what the Powers may want, or into relinquishing her aims.

The way to deal with China is for the Powers to combine and insist on what they want and to go on insisting until they get it.   The Japanese have learnt that.   The European and American Governments often advocate mild measures, but, like the Japanese have done, they, too, will one day find out their mistake.

There are only these alternatives before the Powers.   They must either bring their combined forces to bear on China to get what they want or else leave her alone, until like an awakened lion she is ready to spring on her prey, in which case she will be powerful enough to threaten the acquired rights of all the Powers.

APPENDICES

APPENDIX A

SUMMARY OF THE MEMORIAL OF CHANG-PEI-LUN AND THE BOARD OF CENSORS, 1882.

SINCE the epoch of Tao-Kowan and Shien-Lung our country has been attacked by four calamities. The first of these was the Opium War, the second was the Taiping Rebellion, the third was the Insurrection of the Mohammedans, whilst the fourth is composed of the troubles arising from foreign intercourse.

Since Your Majesty has assumed the direction of the Affairs of State You have by Your supreme ability and the wisdom of Your orders established the strength of the Government, and You have suppressed all difficulties except those arising from our intercourse with foreign nations.

Our foreign relations are of supreme importance and form a very complicated question. But of all our foreign relations, those with Japan cause more trouble than all the others.

The Japanese Government does not enjoy the confidence of its own people, for these reasons. The two principal clans, Satsuma and Choshu, are continually fighting to obtain the predominance in the government, and there are also serious financial difficulties owing to the over-issue of paper. The people in general are very discontented because of the great expenditures on armaments. And it may be remarked that the military system of Japan is not well organized, and the Japanese soldiers may be considered as inferior to the troops at the disposal of Li Hung-Chang and Tsen-Kuo-Fan.

Yet not recognizing her own weaknesses Japan is becoming every year more arrogant towards China, and has even ventured to the seizure of the Loochoo Islands and will seize Korea, as I have humbly pointed out in an earlier memorial. These things, though hard to bear, we have borne with for the sake of peace and in order not to give opportunity for foreigners to again become arrogant towards us.

But now we have had, owing to the actions of Japan, to give the matter further consideration and can no longer restrain our actions to adjust them to the feelings of others. If we do not prepare, then the evil day will be upon us with the swiftness of rain from the sky.

We must check the arrogant claims of Japan and assert once for all time our superiority over her. But this we cannot now do but must make steady preparation. Being ourselves without arrogant designs and having only peaceful intentions we have not armaments suitable or ready to effect this object. Such an undertaking as the defeat of Japan can only be achieved by a preponderating superiority of naval forces. The reorganization and increase of our naval strength are therefore of paramount importance in carrying out our aim.

Meanwhile we must rely on our diplomatic actions. But our diplomacy though directed to suitable ends is ineffective in its results. This is due to the decisions of the Ministers being vague and dilatory, whilst the responsibility of the officials to execute the decisions is limited or irksome.

In my humble opinion, when the Government makes a decision it should also clearly indicate the Minister who shall be responsible for its execution and the general steps he shall adopt in its execution.

And in this matter of our relations with Japan I humbly suggest that Your Majesty should order Your Ministers to discuss and consider the whole, and then after Your Ministers have done so, special officials shall be appointed who shall be responsible for carrying it to a satisfactory conclusion. Only in this way is disaster to be avoided.

And also Li Hung-Chang and Tsen-Kuo-Fan our two most brilliant generals, who established themselves as our leading soldiers by their successes in the Taiping and Mohammedan rebellions, should also be ordered to consider the Japanese affair, and after Your Majesty has received their reports, Your Majesty's supreme wisdom will decide the matter.

But whilst Your Councillors and Ministers are considering this matter, the Viceroys and the Governors of provinces shall make preparation, and complete the naval and military armaments, so that they shall be ready when the time for the conflict with Japan shall come.

It is very important too that the question of the relations between foreign nations and China and Japan be also considered. For in these days the European nations who have established themselves in our land and in Japan consider themselves as of right qualified to decide matters, which in reality

only concern ourselves. We should therefore develop
our friendship with foreign nations so that if it may
be desirable they may help us, or if they should
consider themselves called upon to interfere, then
they should side with us. And this is of the greatest
importance, for I do not think that Japan would be
able to fight with us with the help of a foreign ally.
It is obvious that the strength of Japan compared to
ours is very inferior, and in my humble opinion it is
also evident that she could not obtain foreign assistance so easily as we can. Japan has no close relations
with foreign countries, nor has she any advantages
of commerce which she can offer to them as the price
of assistance in the moment of crisis.

We on the other hand have long and intimate
relations with foreign Powers and every year these
relationships grow closer and warmer. In addition
to this foreign nations want to trade with China,
and we have many important and valuable privileges
which we can offer to them if they assist us when the
time comes. From this it is evident that China can
count with good reason on the assistance of the
foreign Powers in case of war.

The moment for decision has now arrived. Japan
has challenged our rights over Korea, which is our
tributary State, by recognizing the independence of
that country. We certainly have not agreed to this,
and we maintain that Korea is still our tributary
State, but the matter cannot be left so unsettled,
and if we do not assert our rights then by the efflux
of time we may lose them altogether. If we do not
prepare for war, but leave matters in their present
inactive condition, Japan will continue making military and naval preparations whilst we shall be delay-

ing. The power of Japan will be steadily progressing, whilst ours will remain stationary. A Japan stronger than ourselves would be a permanent danger and a continual menace to us. Besides it would have serious consequences upon our relations with the other foreign Powers. Japan is inferior to China in strength and prestige, but if China proves herself unable to crush her then the European Powers will discount their present opinions of us, and the prestige of China will be heavily diminished.

Earlier in the present year I humbly placed my opinion before Your Majesty, and intimated that I suspected Japan of harbouring designs on Korea, and that we should take effective steps to check any further aggression on her part.

Now I am most fully convinced that the suspicions I expressed in that Memorial are correct. I believe the situation is critical, hence I submit to the Throne this my humble opinion, which I trust will receive Your Majesty's most favourable consideration.

CHANG-PEI-LUN
The Board of Censors

The above Memorial was ordered by the Emperor to be submitted to the Board of Military Affairs, which reported on it in entire agreement with the views of Chang-Pei-Lun, and recommending that Li Hung-Chang be appointed to prepare a plan for the invasion of Japan and be appointed to be the responsible Minister for carrying out the plan.

An Imperial Edict to this effect was drawn up and handed to the Board of Military Affairs for transmission to Li Hung-Chang, accompanied by the Memorial from Chang-Pei-Lun.

LI HUNG-CHANG'S MEMORIAL IN REPLY TO THAT OF CHANG-PEI-LUN

I have had the honour of receiving the Imperial Edict of the 16th day of the 7th month, forwarded to me by the Board of Military Affairs and enclosing the memorial of Chang-Pei-Lun, on which I am requested by Your Majesty to express my opinion as to our future relations with Japan.

I entirely agree with the views expressed by Chang-Pei-Lun, that we must prepare for a war with Japan, and therefore we must develop our naval armaments so as to win.

For some years past we have been so engaged, keeping this object in view, and great efforts have been made to reorganize our army and navy. Enormous sums have been spent in order to enable us to display our superiority and assert our power over our neighbour, whenever the favourable moment for the conflict shall have arrived.

The Convention lately concluded between Korea and Japan is merely the consequence of the attack on the Japanese Legation at Seoul, committed by conspirators, and which was followed by a massacre of Japanese residents at that place. We have no right to interfere on this question.

In the treaty between Korea and Japan the latter recognizes Korea as an independent State, without any regard to us. But respecting this we must remember that China has never recognized Korea as an independent State, in which course other Powers have agreed with us, and this has led them to assume an attitude opposed to Japan.

Our best case for causing a rupture with Japan

is not over the Korean question but in regard to the
Loochoo Islands. We have an indisputable right to
these islands, and every foreign Power would have
to admit our claim, if we demand the restoration of
our rights over them.

The actual situation in Japan is that the country
is labouring under financial difficulties and suffering
from the burden of a terrible national debt. The
struggles between Satsuma and Choshu, the two chief
political parties, affect its power and the present
weakness of the army and navy is admitted.

Japan, ever since the restoration, has tried her
best to make good understandings with foreign nations, and Japan hopes to preserve her independence
by means of foreign influence exerted in her favour.

It is for this reason that the Japanese Government
has this year sent the Chief Minister of State, Ito
Hironobu, to Europe, ostensibly to inquire into the
systems of administration. Prince Arisugawa of
the Imperial House has been sent to Russia to visit
the Imperial Court there. This year two diplomatic
missions have been established in Italy and Austria.
These servile efforts of Japan to promote international
intercourse have created a good impression abroad.
Her envoys have been well received, and in my opinion, the Powers will help Japan to a certain extent.
I think that in the event of a conflict between China
and Japan, the foreign Powers would be on her side.

But let us remember that the two great principles
which exercise paramount influence in the world
are reason and strength. The former is a moral
power, the latter is material. The former distin-
guishes between right and wrong, the latter makes
might into right, when opposed to weakness.

Morally we have an undoubted right to the Loochoo Islands, and materially China is a large and strong Empire, superior to Japan. If we only organize our resources, develop our army and navy we shall gain the respect of even the more powerful of foreign nations, who will rank us with the Great Powers, and then Japan will not even venture to carry out any hostile designs against us.

But if Japan should prematurely discover our plans to make a war against her, then her Government and people will be reunited, she will ally with a foreign Power, accumulate money by issuing loans, increase her army and navy, build and purchase warships, with the result that we should be in a disadvantageous position, pregnant with danger.

An ancient maxim says: "Nothing is so dangerous as to expose one's plans before they are ripe." It is for this reason that I recommended to Your Majesty that we maintain extreme caution, carefully concealing our object whilst all the time increasing our strength. Success or failure depends entirely on a favourable moment being chosen to put our plans into execution. No man however experienced or distinguished can hope to achieve success if he strikes at the wrong time.

Japan has since many years followed the Western systems, and though her success may not altogether be conceded, her fleet, it cannot be denied, is the equal of ours. I therefore think it would be hazardous to send our fleet into Japanese waters to fight. Whilst we should not lose sight of the plan for the invasion of Japan, we should not make the mistake of hurrying the invasion. In my humble opinion we must first reorganize the navy before we even think of an invasion of Japan.

Your Majesty has ordered me to prepare a plan of invasion and be responsible for its execution.   Humbly I submit that this plan must be one of the most important questions for the future of the Empire and is not the work of one man.   Such a plan must end in failure unless the Viceroys and Governors of all Provinces work together earnestly and harmoniously for many years to ensure its success.

During the Taiping Revolution the Government ordered the various Viceroys to crush the rebels, each being responsible for their defeat in his own province, and allowed to use the resources of his own province.   The result was that the rebellion spread, because the action of the Viceroys was limited and hampered.   When the Government saw this it changed its plans, and instead of dividing the power and limiting the authority of each Viceroy, they were ordered to co-operate and work together.   The result was immediately visible, for as the result of the great efforts, rebellion was completely suppressed.   But this was due to the possibility of massing troops and supplies in sufficient quantities and the stricter control over subordinates.

Now the present is a period of tranquillity, and the ancient laws and regulations are everywhere honoured, so that our Government service is only open to men who have obtained distinction in the literary examinations.   But being limited for candidates to the examination halls, there is great difficulty in obtaining suitable persons, and in my humble opinion this condition should be altered, so we obtain men who though not great scholars will yet be capable administrators.

Again we must make early and suitable arrangements with the various Viceroys and Governors for the provision of supplies and material, and this will need much time and work.

I think it is essential, if it is desired to obtain the services of suitable persons, that quite another method of entry into the public services must be initiated. That would alter the present examination system.

And to secure the harmonious co-operation of the Viceroys and Governors of provinces we must abolish their semi-independence and secure joint action from them.

Let the Ministers and Viceroys agree together and let Your Majesty instruct them in accordance with Your august decisions, and then the scheme to invade Japan will be possible of execution.

But even so it is most inadvisable to place the responsibility of the invasion on my shoulders alone.

What Chang-Pei-Lun says of the ill-success of diplomatic action, the indefinite nature of the Ministerial decisions, and the lack of official responsibility, is true and indisputable!

As an example I humbly submit that the necessity of building a strong navy and the decision to build new warships therefor was fully agreed upon by all Ministers and Viceroys, and the Minister of Finance ordered an annual appropriation of Tls. 4,000,000 to form a fund to cover the naval expenditure and the cost of coastal defences. This amount must be debited to the revenue of the Inland Customs, but unfortunately the estimate of revenue was wrong, and in most provinces the cost of collection exceeded the receipts. In Fukien and Kwantung the amounts collected were spent locally instead of being remitted to the Imperial Treasury.

My department as a consequence received barely a quarter of the Tls. 4,000,000 appropriated to it, with the natural result that the growth of the navy and the organization of the coastal defence was hindered.

I humbly hope Your Majesty will order the Imperial Treasury and the Department of Foreign Affairs to prepare an accurate estimate of the contributions due from each province for defence purposes, and an additional amount will be granted for the defence of Formosa. Any deficiency in the Provincial contribution should be balanced from the Imperial Treasury so that an annual amount of Tls. 4,000,000 be available for the navy and coastal defence. With this annual sum I will in five years provide a strong navy and reorganize our coastal defences.

As Formosa and Shantung are the parts of the Empire most liable to attack, our most capable generals should be selected for their defences.

I summarize my humble opinion as follows:

(1) It is essential to strengthen the national defences.

(2) It is essential to organize a strong navy.

(3) There is no hurry to attack Japan.

LI HUNG-CHANG.

It was as a result of Chang-Pei-Lun's memorial and the recommendations of Prince Ch'un, the Emperor's father, that Li was in 1885 ordered to undertake the necessary measures for the naval defence of China. A Board of Admiralty was created with Prince Ch'un as President, and Li as Associate

Vice-President and Treasurer. A Naval College
was founded on the system of competitive examination, and Prince Ch'un and Li visited a British warship at Port Arthur. Chang-Pei-Lun commanded a
squadron which was defeated by the French off Foo-
chow and was twice cashiered for speculation and
misbehaviour. He was described as a man of rare
force of character but of evil habits, which got
unlimited scope after 1888 when he married Li's
daughter.

¹ A translation of a considerable portion of the Chang memorial
and of the whole of Li's comment appeared in the London
Times in January, 1895.—ED.

APPENDIX B

ANGLO-JAPANESE ALLIANCE

(Concluded Jan. 30, 1902)

ART. I. The High Contracting Parties, having mutually recognized the independence of China and Korea, declare themselves to be entirely uninfluenced by any aggressive tendencies in either country. Having in view, however, their special interests, of which those of Great Britain relate principally to China, while Japan, in addition to the interests which she possesses in China, is interested in a peculiar degree politically, as well as commercially and industrially, in Korea, the High Contracting Parties recognize that it will be admissible for either of them to take such measures as may be indispensable in order to safeguard those interests if threatened either by the aggressive action of any other Power, or by disturbances arising in China or Korea, and necessitating the intervention of either of the High Contracting Parties for the protection of the lives and property of its subjects.

ART. II. If either Great Britain or Japan, in the defence of their respective interests as above described, should become involved in war with another Power, the other High Contracting Party will maintain a strict neutrality, and use its efforts to prevent others from joining in hostilities against its ally.

ART. III. If in the above event any other Power or Powers should join in hostilities against that ally, the other High Contracting Party will come to its assistance, and will conduct the war in common, and make peace in mutual agreement with it.

ART. IV. The High Contracting Parties agree that neither of them will, without consulting the other, enter into separate arrangements with another Power to the prejudice of the interests above described.

ART. V. Whenever, in the opinion of either Great Britain or Japan, the above-mentioned interests are in jeopardy, the two Governments will communicate with one another fully and frankly.

ART. VI. The present Agreement shall come into effect immediately after the date of its signature, and remain in force for five years from that date. In case neither of the High Contracting Parties should have notified twelve months before the expiration of the said five years the intention of terminating it, it shall remain binding until the expiration of one year from the day on which either of the High Contracting Parties shall have denounced it. But if when the date fixed for its expiration arrives either ally is actually engaged in war, the alliance shall *ipso facto* continue until peace is concluded.

APPENDIX C

THE FRANCO-JAPANESE AGREEMENT

The Government of His Majesty the Emperor of Japan and the Government of the French Republic, animated by the desire to strengthen the relations of amity existing between them and to remove from those relations all cause of misunderstanding for the future, have decided to conclude the following Arrangement.

"The Governments of Japan and France, being agreed to respect the independence and integrity of China, as well as the principle of equal treatment in that country for the commerce and subjects or citizens of all nations, and having a special interest to have the order and pacific state of things preserved especially in the regions of the Chinese Empire adjacent to the territories where they have the rights of sovereignty, protection, or occupation, engage to support each other for assuring the peace and security in those regions, with a view to maintain the respective situation and the territorial rights of the two High Contracting Parties in the Continent of Asia."

In witness whereof, the Undersigned: His Excellency Monsieur Kurino, Ambassador Extraordinary and Plenipotentiary of Japan to the President of the French Republic, and His Excellency Monsieur

Stephen Pichon, Senator, Minister for Foreign Affairs, authorized by their respective Governments, have signed this Arrangement and have affixed thereto their seals.

Done at Paris, the 10th of June, 1907.

(L.S.) S. KURINO.
(L.S.) S. PICHON.

APPENDIX D

THE RUSSO-JAPANESE CONVENTION

CONVENTION

THE Government of His Majesty the Emperor of Japan and the Government of His Majesty the Emperor of All The Russias, desirous of consolidating the peaceful and friendly relations, which have been so happily re-established between Japan and Russia, and wishing to avert for the future all cause of misunderstanding in the relations of the two Empires, have agreed on the following conditions:

ARTICLE I

Each of the High Contracting Parties pledges itself to respect the present territorial integrity of the other and all the rights accruing to either party from the treaties, conventions, and contracts in force between them and China, copies of which have been exchanged between the Contracting Parties (in so far as these rights are not incompatible with the principle of equal opportunity) and from the Treaty signed at Portsmouth on September 5th (23d August, Old Style), 1905, as well as the special conventions concluded between Japan and Russia.

ARTICLE II

The Two High Contracting Parties recognize the independence and territorial integrity of the Empire of China and the principle of equal opportunity in that which concerns the commerce and industry of all the nations in that Empire, and pledge themselves to sustain and defend the maintenance of the *status quo* and respect for this principle by all pacific means in their power.

In witness whereof the undersigned, being authorized by their respective Governments, have signed this convention and have affixed thereto their seals.

Done at St. Petersburg, the 30th day of the seventh month, of the 40th year of Meiji, corresponding to the 17th (30th) July, 1907.

(L.S.)   I. MOTONO.
(L.S).   ISWOLSKY.

APPENDIX E

THE AMERICAN-JAPANESE AGREEMENT

NOTES

Exchanged between the JAPANESE AMBASSADOR *at Washington and the* SECRETARY OF STATE *of the United States.*

From the JAPANESE AMBASSADOR *to the* SECRETARY OF STATE

JAPANESE EMBASSY,
WASHINGTON, *November 30,* 1908.

SIR,—The exchange of views between us which has taken place at the several interviews which I have recently had the honour of holding with you, has shown that Japan and the United States holding important outlying insular possessions in the region of the Pacific Ocean, the Governments of the two countries are animated by a common aim, policy, and intention in that region.

Believing that a frank avowal of that aim, policy, and intention would not only tend to strengthen the relations of friendship and good neighbourhood which have immemorially existed between Japan and

329

the United States, but would materially contribute to the preservation of the general peace, the Imperial Government have authorized me to present to you an outline of their understanding of that common aim, policy, and intention.

(1) It is the wish of the two Governments to encourage the free and peaceful development of their commerce on the Pacific Ocean;

(2) The policy of both Governments, uninfluenced by any aggressive tendencies, is directed to the maintenance of the existing *status quo* in the region above mentioned and to the defence of the principle of equal opportunity for commerce and industry in China;

(3) They are accordingly firmly resolved reciprocally to respect the territorial possessions belonging to each other in said region;

(4) They are also determined to preserve the common interests of all Powers in China, by supporting, by all pacific means at their disposal, the independence and integrity of China and the principle of equal opportunity for commerce and industry of all nations in that Empire;

(5) Should any event occur threatening the *status quo* as above described or the principle of equal opportunity as above defined, it remains for the two Governments to communicate with each other as to what measures they may consider it useful to take.

If the foregoing outline accords with the view of the Government of the United States, I shall be gratified to receive your confirmation.

I take, etc., etc.,

K. TAKAHIRA.

From the SECRETARY OF STATE *to the*
JAPANESE AMBASSADOR

DEPARTMENT OF STATE,
WASHINGTON, *November* 30, 1908.

EXCELLENCY,—I have the honour to acknowledge
the receipt of your Note of to-day, setting forth the
result of the exchange of views between us in our
recent interviews, defining the understanding of the
two Governments in regard to their policy in the
region of the Pacific Ocean.

It is a pleasure to inform you that this expression
of mutual understanding is welcome to the Government of the United States as appropriate to the happy
relations of the two countries and as the occasion of
a concise mutual affirmation of that accordant policy
respecting the Far East, which the two Governments
have so frequently declared in the past.

I am happy to be able to inform Your Excellency,
on behalf of the United States, of the declaration of
the two Governments embodied in the following
words:

[Here follows a declaration identical with that
given by Baron Takahira, and the signature of Mr.
Elihu Root.]

DATE DUE

4/16			